TURNING POINTS

I0808594

By Joseph Stanley

THE CREATION OF ISIS

Cavendish Square
New York

Published in 2022 by Cavendish Square Publishing,
29 East 21st Street,
New York, NY 10010

Copyright © 2022 by Cavendish Square Publishing, LLC

First Edition

No part of this publication may be reproduced, stored in a retrieval system, or transmitted in any form or by any means—electronic, mechanical, photocopying, recording, or otherwise—without the prior permission of the copyright owner. Request for permission should be addressed to Permissions, Cavendish Square Publishing, 243 5th Avenue, Suite 136, New York, NY 10016. Tel (877) 980-4450; fax (877) 980-4454.

Website: cavendishsq.com

This publication represents the opinions and views of the author based on his or her personal experience, knowledge, and research. The information in this book serves as a general guide only. The author and publisher have used their best efforts in preparing this book and disclaim liability rising directly or indirectly from the use and application of this book.

Portions of this work were originally authored by Caroline Kennon and published as *The Rise of ISIS: The Modern Age of Terrorism* (*World History*). All new material this edition authored by Joseph Stanley.

All websites were available and accurate when this book was sent to press.

Library of Congress Cataloging-in-Publication Data

Names: Stanley, Joseph, author.
Title: The creation of ISIS / Joseph Stanley.
Description: New York : Cavendish Square Publishing, 2022. | Series: Turning points | Includes bibliographical references and index.
Identifiers: LCCN 2020025208 | ISBN 9781502660756 (library binding) | ISBN 9781502660749 (paperback) | ISBN 9781502660763 (ebook)
Subjects: LCSH: ISIS (Organization)–Juvenile literature. | Terrorism–Religious aspects–Islam–Juvenile literature. | Islamic fundamentalism–History–Juvenile literature. | Middle East–History–21st century–Juvenile literature.
Classification: LCC HV6433.I722 S73 2022 | DDC 363.3250956–dc23
LC record available at https://lccn.loc.gov/2020025208

Editor: Katie Kawa
Copy Editor: Abby Young
Designer: Deanna Paternostro

Some of the images in this book illustrate individuals who are models. The depictions do not imply actual situations or events.

CPSIA compliance information: Batch #CS22CSQ: For further information contact Cavendish Square Publishing LLC, New York, New York at 1-877-980-4450.

Printed in the United States of America

Find us on

TABLE OF CONTENTS

INTRODUCTION

THE ISLAMIC STATE

On October 27, 2019, U.S. president Donald Trump addressed the nation to deliver an important message to the American people: "Last night, the United States brought the world's No. 1 terrorist leader to justice. Abu Bakr al-Baghdadi is dead."[1]

Why was the death of one man in another country such important news for Americans? At the time of his death, al-Baghdadi was known as the leader of the Islamic State in Iraq and Syria, which is most commonly known as ISIS and is one of the most infamous terrorist organizations in the world. The group has also been known by other names, including the Islamic State in Iraq and the Levant (ISIL) and Daesh. No matter what name it is called, its impact on the world has been undeniable. ISIS has claimed responsibility for directly carrying out and inspiring terrorist attacks around the world that have left thousands of people dead. Many of these attacks have been carried out by people who were influenced by ISIS propaganda on the internet, which has given this terrorist organization a global platform for its message of violent Islamist extremism.

Although ISIS has declined in power in recent years, its creation and rise to global infamy marked a turning point in the modern

Shown here is ISIS leader Abu Bakr al-Baghdadi before his death on October 26, 2019. He oversaw ISIS as it grew into one of the world's most feared terrorist groups, and his death was seen as a major victory in the global fight against terrorism.

age of terrorism. Understanding its goals, its methods, and its rapid growth can shed a light on the reasons why people around the world might be inspired to commit horrific acts of violence in the name of one group and its beliefs.

What Does ISIS Want?

ISIS is sometimes known simply as the Islamic State, and that name also clearly indicates the main goal of this terrorist group. It believes that it is meant to create and spread an Islamic state, or caliphate, that is governed by sharia law, which is the system of rules based on the Muslim holy book known as the Quran. While most Muslims interpret the Quran and sharia law in a peaceful way that encourages them to live good lives and have strong morals, followers of ISIS believe that they are called to spread sharia law through conquest, eliminating anything and anyone that stands in the way of expanding the caliphate to cover the entire world. This includes all other religions, including Christianity and Judaism.

The leader of a caliphate is called a caliph, so this is what the leader of ISIS is known as to its followers. They believe the caliph is meant to follow in the footsteps of Muhammad, who is known as the most important prophet in the Muslim faith. He worked to spread the religion in the seventh century CE and served as both a religious and political leader. The caliphs who have followed continue this leadership, although support for caliphs throughout history has not been universal. This is especially true for the leaders of ISIS who have called themselves caliphs and have called the territory they've claimed a caliphate. Most Muslims around the world strongly stand against the message and methods of ISIS and do not follow its leaders or consider them to be caliphs.

Islam's Basic Beliefs

The actions of violent terrorist groups that claim to follow Islam, such as ISIS, have led some people to see Islam as a violent and repressive belief system. Islamophobia—hatred and fear of people who follow Islam—has become a major concern in countries such as the United States, and the actions of groups such as ISIS often make non-Muslims more afraid of and prejudiced against all who practice the Muslim faith. However, a closer look at the realities of Islam and the beliefs of ordinary Muslims around the world reveals that there is a huge difference between what ISIS and other extremist groups preach and what most followers of Islam practice.

Islam is an Arabic word that translates to "submission" or "surrender" in English and refers to surrendering to the will of God, who is known to Muslims as Allah. Like Christianity and Judaism, Islam is monotheistic, which means its followers believe in only one God. These three religions also share a series of important figures and prophets sent by God, including Abraham and Jesus. Muslims believe that Muhammad, who was born around 570 CE in Mecca in what's now Saudi Arabia, is the most important prophet.

The belief in Allah and Muhammad makes up the first of the five pillars of Islam—the core beliefs and practices that Muslims are called to follow. The *shahadah* is the Muslim profession of faith: "There is no god but Allah, and Muhammad is his messenger." The second pillar of Islam is the *salat*, which is the daily prayer that must be performed five times a day facing the direction of the holy city of Mecca. The third pillar is *zakat*, which is the paying of a tax to help the poor. The fourth is *sawm*, which is the fasting that must be done during the month of Ramadan. Ramadan is the ninth month of the Islamic calendar and is when Muhammad is thought to have received the first of the revelations written in the Quran. Muslims can't eat or drink during daylight hours during Ramadan. The fifth and final pillar is the *hajj*, which is the pilgrimage to Mecca that every Muslim must make once in their life if possible.

Islam is the world's fastest-growing religion, and more than a billion people around the world practice it. These people follow different branches of Islam. The largest group is the Sunnis. ISIS is made up of Sunni Muslims, but followers of ISIS make up a very small percentage of this group overall. In the eyes of ISIS, some of their biggest enemies are Shia (also called Shiite) Muslims. The biggest difference between these two groups is that the Sunnis believe the first four caliphs after Muhammad's death were legitimate successors to Muhammad. The Shia, however, believe only the fourth caliph,

Muslims around the world have condemned the actions of ISIS and other Islamist terrorist groups. "Islamist" is a word that is often used to refer to militant or extremist interpretations of Islam.

Ali, and his descendants are the rightful successors to Muhammad, and they reject the first three caliphs. Although most Islamic violence happening in the Middle East revolves around these two denominations, there are also some additional smaller groups, including the Wahhabi, a Sunni sect in Saudi Arabia and Qatar, and the Alawites, a Syrian Shia sect that observes some Christian holidays in addition to traditional Islamic ones.

Although Muslims share basic beliefs, the actions of one group do not speak for them all. This is especially true when contrasting the actions of ISIS with the more peaceful and inclusive interpretation of Islam practiced by most Muslims around the world. In fact, a 2017 study conducted by the Pew Research Center revealed that an overwhelming majority of Muslims reject the violent extremism of groups such as ISIS.

Extremism and Terrorism

Although most Muslims don't support the kind of violent extremism practiced by ISIS, the prevalence of Islamist violence in the news has led many to falsely connect those actions with Islam as a whole. For example, both Muslims and Western media frequently refer to the word "jihad." Literally, this word means the struggle of an individual to follow Allah's commands, both at a personal and community level. However, it has been associated in modern times with radical

Islam and the fight against those who do not follow Islam, and the word "jihadist" is now often used to refer to an Islamist militant. It is important to note that the original teachings of Islam do not encourage jihadist violence.

Jihadist violence is typically considered a form of terrorism—the use or threat of violence to intimidate other people or governments, often to achieve a political or social goal. ISIS has attempted to terrorize the Western world—meaning countries, such as the United States and much of Europe, that have roots in the ancient Greek and Roman civilizations and in Christianity—by killing and threatening in order to eventually achieve its goal of a global caliphate.

Modern international terrorism that is rooted in religious differences is typically traced back to the 1960s, when Palestinians, who are mostly Muslim, realized they could not fight the much larger Israeli (mostly Jewish) military. When Palestinians realized they would not win with traditional warfare, many started using urban terrorist methods. Radical Palestinians hijacked planes, kidnapped civilians, and bombed Israelis in a way that became a model for other small ethnic and religious movements.

In 1979, the Soviet Union invaded Afghanistan. This ignited a war that lasted until 1989 and sparked the creation of many terrorist groups. The Afghan people could not take on the Soviet Union outright, but they could attack in very small numbers through bombings and kidnappings, which weakened the Soviets' will to fight. Volunteers from all over the Islamic world fought for Afghanistan. After the Soviets left that country in 1989, it became a popular location to train terrorists. The terrorist group al-Qaeda is the most famous group that benefited from this environment.

Terrorism became coordinated and widespread with the creation of the Taliban, an Islamist political movement in Afghanistan. Since 1989, Islamist terrorist organizations have also attacked targets well outside of their geographic areas. For example, on September 11, 2001, Islamist terrorists crashed planes into the World Trade Center in New York City and the Pentagon outside of Washington, D.C., as well as into a field in Pennsylvania, killing nearly 3,000 people.

Memorials to the victims of terrorist attacks are found around the world. Shown here is a memorial in Paris, France, for the victims of a series of coordinated terrorist attacks in November 2015 that left 130 people dead. ISIS claimed responsibility for those attacks.

Ever since the events of September 11, 2001, which is also referred to as 9/11, terrorism has been linked with Islamist extremism in the eyes of many Americans, although in the United States, terrorist attacks are more often carried out by people who are not Muslim. ISIS has kept the focus of the media on Islamist extremism through its methods of public executions and other forms of brutal violence, including kidnappings, beheadings, and bombings in Iraq, Syria, and other parts of the world.

A Rapid Rise and Fall

Today, the media's attention—and, as such, the public's focus—on ISIS isn't as strong as it once was. This is because the group isn't as powerful as it was at its peak. In 2014, ISIS controlled more than 34,000 square miles (88,000 square kilometers) in Syria and Iraq. This location was important because, according to Islamic prophecy, Dabiq, Syria, is where the final battle between the Muslim world and the West is supposed to take place before the end of the world. Those leading ISIS want to be on the front lines when that final battle begins.

By 2015, however, ISIS was starting to lose its territory, which was a problem for a group that needed a physical location for its caliphate. Two years later, it had lost around 95 percent of the lands it had once claimed, and two years after that, its leader was dead.

Despite these victories in the battle against ISIS and claims that the group has been defeated for good, the fight is far from over. A new leader was appointed after al-Baghdadi's death, and in 2020 and 2021, ISIS captured headlines again by staging attacks on military and civilian targets in Iraq.

By looking back to the creation of ISIS, we can better understand the conditions that caused this organization to form and rise to prominence. This understanding is an important part of the fight against terrorism around the world.

CHAPTER ONE

AL-QAEDA IN IRAQ

Tracing the roots of ISIS is a complex process. It involves looking deeply into wars, religious divisions, and cultural tensions in the Middle East and Afghanistan—as well as that region's relationship with the West—stretching back more than 40 years. Political, economic, and social instability in this part of the world has left many people—especially many young men—angry and looking for a way to turn their anger into action. In some cases, they have turned to terrorist groups to give them a sense of purpose and a leader to follow.

Leadership is an important part of Islamist terrorist organizations such as ISIS. There is often a clear chain of command, and if the leader is killed, another person can step up to fill that role. This keeps the organization going. It also allows for one person to serve as the face and voice of the organization.

The story of the creation of ISIS begins with one such leader: Osama bin Laden.

An Outsider in His Own Family

In 1957, the 17th child of Muhammad bin Awad bin Laden was born in Saudi Arabia. His name was Osama bin Muhammad bin Awad bin Laden. Muhammad bin Laden was an immigrant to Saudi Arabia from Yemen and a self-made billionaire. He was the owner of a very

Osama bin Laden was the founder of the Islamist terrorist organization al-Qaeda. ISIS can trace its roots back to this extremist group, which was responsible for the 9/11 terrorist attacks.

successful construction company—so successful that it is credited with the restorations and extensions of the three most holy mosques in Islam: al-Aqsa, Mecca, and Medina.

Muhammad bin Laden was a polygamist, which means he was married to multiple women at the same time. This custom is legal in Saudi Arabia but illegal in many other countries, such as the United States. Osama's mother was from Syria, and Osama was her only child. It was highly unusual for rich and powerful Saudis to be born to two parents from outside the kingdom. The country of Saudi Arabia believes that family history is important, and Osama must have felt like an outsider because neither of his parents could claim Saudi Arabian ancestry.

In 1967, tragedy shook the family when Muhammad died in a plane crash. Osama was only 10 years old. Although there were more than 50 bin Laden children, each sibling inherited millions of dollars. Their lives were similar to the lives of celebrities or royalty, and the family had a close relationship with the Saudi royal family.

Osama bin Laden grew up as a dedicated Muslim. Like most Saudis, he grew up around Wahhabism, which is a conservative branch of Islam that shuns Western ways of life. While earning his college degree at King Abdul Aziz University in Saudi Arabia, he became involved with Islamic extremists and also learned marketing skills that he would one day use to recruit fellow extremists to his cause.

The Rise of the Mujahideen

Osama bin Laden first gained a reputation as a militant Islamist leader during the war between the Soviet Union and Afghanistan. Near the end of 1979, the Union of Soviet Socialist Republics, or Soviet Union (which eventually broke up, creating separate nations, including Russia), crossed the border into neighboring Afghanistan to establish control. The groups of anti-Soviet Afghan fighters were collectively named the mujahideen, or "those who do jihad," and they tried to prevent the Soviets from taking over their government. Soon after the invasion of Afghanistan, Osama bin Laden began meeting with members of the Afghan resistance and raising money to help their cause.

Osama bin Laden wasn't the only person interested in sending resources to help the mujahideen. In fact, the United States and bin Laden were actually on the same side of the fight. The United States helped Afghanistan fight the Soviets during the invasion by supplying

During the 1970s and 1980s, the United States and the Soviet Union were on opposite sides of a global conflict known as the Cold War. This is why the United States sided with the mujahideen (*shown here*) after the Soviets invaded Afghanistan.

weapons and money to the mujahideen. It has been argued by some that the U.S. government helped extremist groups in Afghanistan grow by giving them weapons and money.

Over the next nine years, the Soviet Union occupied Afghanistan while the mujahideen fighters, aided by bin Laden, tried to push them out. More than 1 million Afghan citizens and more than 14,500 Soviet soldiers were killed in the fighting, which ended when the Soviet Union removed its last troops from Afghanistan in 1989. This war paved the way for the birth of the Taliban, which rose to power in 1996, by leaving Afghanistan incredibly vulnerable. It also led to the formation of al-Qaeda.

Al-Qaeda vs. America

By the time the Soviet Union left Afghanistan in 1989, the damage was done. The country and the entire region had become unsettled, and the environment was perfect for the rise of terrorist groups—chief among them being al-Qaeda. This network actually grew from a database that bin Laden used to compile information about Afghan resistance soldiers. In 1988, it became an organized group of extremists with a strong recruiting base. For these recruits, bin Laden himself became a larger-than-life figure: a young man who had transformed from a rich boy to a warrior. However, intelligence sources say he only saw combat very briefly. Regardless, his reputation was one of his most important assets, and it led to more recruits.

Bin Laden eventually met Ayman al-Zawahiri, an Egyptian surgeon who would become his right-hand man. In 1998, bin Laden and al-Zawahiri announced that their individual terrorist organizations—al-Qaeda and the Egyptian Islamic Jihad, respectively—would become a single organization.

Now presenting a powerful and dangerous front, their combined forces issued the following fatwa (decree based on an interpretation of Islamic law): "The judgment to kill and fight Americans and their allies, whether civilians or military, is an obligation for every Muslim."[1] They hated the United States because it chose to back non-Islamic leaders in Israel and Egypt, and they saw the Western way of life—represented by Americans—as one that was in strict opposition to the true ways of Islam. Although the United States and bin Laden had once fought on the same side, that time was over. Al-Qaeda and other terrorist groups instructed their followers to cause as much damage as possible to U.S. targets.

An Unlikely Leader in the Levant

Al-Qaeda's reputation reached far and wide among radical groups in the Middle East. In 1999, the Jordanian extremist Abu Musab al-Zarqawi (who was born Ahmad Fadil Nazal al-Khalayleh but changed his name later in life) traveled to Afghanistan to ask Osama bin Laden for money and help training terrorists. Although al-Zarqawi was looking to bin Laden for funding, they had one major difference in beliefs. Al-Zarqawi passionately disliked the Shia sect of Islam, but bin Laden's own mother was a member of this sect. Al-Zarqawi wanted to bring glory to the Sunnis while destroying the Shia, but bin Laden believed that Muslims should all work together to fight against the West. Despite this difference, bin Laden decided to support al-Zarqawi because al-Qaeda had so few allies from Jordan. Bin Laden's advisors also saw merit in al-Zarqawi's focus on the part of the world known as the Levant—an area around the Mediterranean Sea that includes Syria, Lebanon, Israel, Palestine, and Jordan.

Although both al-Zarqawi and bin Laden shared many extremist Muslim views and became known as leaders of the Islamist terrorism movement, their lives had almost nothing in common. Bin Laden was a college graduate from a very wealthy and influential family; Ahmad Fadil Nazal al-Khalayleh was born in a poor part of the industrial city of Zarqa, Jordan. It is from the name of this city that Ahmad took the name al-Zarqawi. He felt a lot of affection for his hometown; until he died, he kept a house in Zarqa.

Al-Zarqawi would one day become known as the founder of ISIS, but nothing about his young adult days hinted at his future as an Islamist terrorist organizer. He was a wild teenager. He had the reputation of being a bully and a thug. He was a heavy drinker and was constantly getting into fights. When he was 15, he robbed a relative's home, and he dropped out of high school in his final year. Al-Zarqawi grew up to become a petty criminal who was covered in tattoos, including a distinctive green tattoo

Shown here is the city of Zarqa, the hometown and namesake of Abu Musab al-Zarqawi.

on his left hand. He was in and out of prison many times.

In 1989, al-Zarqawi arrived in Afghanistan and stayed for an extended period of time, establishing contacts. He was hired as the correspondent for a jihadist magazine called *Al-Bonian al-Marsous*, or *The Strong Wall*. Eventually, he began attending jihadist training camps on the Afghanistan-Pakistan border.

Finding Allies

Al-Zarqawi returned to Jordan in the early 1990s and was introduced to Abu Muhammad al-Maqdisi, an intelligent Salafist who practiced the most extreme version of the Islamic movement known as Salafism, which is based on hatred of Shia Muslims and Western culture and on a literal interpretation of the Quran. Al-Maqdisi became al-Zarqawi's mentor and a tremendous influence on him.

The research director of the Combating Terrorism Center at West Point, Jarret Brachman, said:

> *It's not surprising that Zarqawi embraced Salafism. Jihadi Salafism is black and white—and so is everything that Zarqawi's ever done. When he met al-Maqdisi, he was drifting, trying to find an outlet, and very impressionable [easy to influence]. His religious grounding, until then, was largely dependent upon whose influence he was under at the time. And since his father had died when he was young, he'd been seeking a father figure. Al-Maqdisi served both needs.*[2]

Back in Jordan, al-Zarqawi also met Abu Muntassir, an experienced Islamist militant. Muntassir taught al-Zarqawi about militant Islamism, and eventually, al-Zarqawi approached him about plans to form an Islamist extremist group. Muntassir recounted, "Zarqawi asked me to work with him in an Islamic group; al-Maqdisi was already on board. The idea was there, but it had no leadership and no name."[3] The group that al-Zarqawi, al-Maqdisi, and Muntassir formed consisted of about a dozen men who wanted to overthrow the

Jordanian monarchy and establish an Islamic government. However, it was not yet a well-oiled machine.

Becoming a Leader in Prison

This group called itself Bayat al-Imam, which means "Allegiance to the Imam." (An imam is a high-ranking Muslim religious official.) According to one report, the group sent one of its men to blow up a local movie theater in Zarqa because it was showing inappropriate films. The bomber, however, was distracted by the film and ended up blowing his own legs off. Later, the Jordanian military raided al-Zarqawi's family home and found a stockpile of weapons, including grenades. Charged with possession of illegal weapons and belonging to a terrorist organization, he was sentenced to 15 years in Jordan's Swaqa Prison.

The time he spent in prison shaped al-Zarqawi into the man who would establish ISIS years later. He held a lot of authority over other prisoners, made connections, and developed credibility as a radical Islamic leader. He used his time in prison to memorize all the verses of the Quran. New recruits were drawn to him—some because they were inspired and others because they were afraid.

A fellow prisoner of al-Zarqawi's, Abdullah Abu Rumman, said that al-Zarqawi "decided who would cook, who would do the laundry, who would lead the readings of the Koran [an alternate spelling of Quran]. He was extremely protective of his followers, and extremely tough with prisoners outside his group. He didn't trust them. He considered them infidels [people outside of his religion]."[4]

Its leaders being in prison did not slow the growth of Bayat al-Imam; it expanded both inside and outside the prison. Al-Zarqawi recruited, and al-Maqdisi, who was also imprisoned, preached. They used the internet to spread their message across continents, which would become one of the most infamous tactics ISIS has used to recruit and inspire followers around the world.

In 1999, Jordan's king died, and his son pardoned more than 3,000 prisoners. After serving less than half of his sentence, al-Zarqawi was freed.

Fighting in Afghanistan

That first meeting between al-Zarqawi and bin Laden took place after his release from prison in 1999. A former Israeli intelligence official described it as "loathing at first sight."[5] As such, al-Zarqawi was rejected as a candidate for official membership in al-Qaeda. However, in 2000, al-Zarqawi was given money to develop a training camp in Herat, Afghanistan.

By 2001, al-Zarqawi had evolved from an unsophisticated thug into a military commander. He even joined forces with al-Qaeda and the Taliban to fight against the United States in Afghanistan. American forces began air strikes in Afghanistan in October 2001, a little less than a month after al-Qaeda carried out the 9/11 attacks. Al-Zarqawi eventually left Afghanistan for Iran before making the move to Iraq, which would ultimately lead to the creation of ISIS.

International Infamy

As al-Zarqawi was getting to Iraq, on the other side of the world, he was being recognized by the United States as a growing threat. The Central Intelligence Agency (CIA) proposed that he be targeted in order to prevent any future problems. They created a plan of attack that would take al-Zarqawi out of the picture for good. They were shocked when President George W. Bush and Vice President Dick Cheney did not approve their action and instead used al-Zarqawi as a link between Osama bin Laden and Saddam Hussein.

Saddam Hussein was the dictator of Iraq and a Sunni Muslim. He became the president in 1979 and, sharing al-Zarqawi's feelings about Shia Muslims, expelled 40,000 of them from the country. Until the Americans took control of Iraq in 2003 and his execution in 2006, Hussein continued a reign of terror and death against his own Iraqi people. He was also known around the world for attempting to develop nuclear and biological weapons. After the 9/11 terror attacks, the White House tried to link Saddam Hussein to al-Qaeda, but they were unable to. In 2003, though, al-Zarqawi was entering Iraq with a history of terrorism and a seemingly strong link to al-Qaeda. To some U.S. government officials, he seemed like the link between Afghanistan-based al-Qaeda and the Iraqi leader.

The two biggest problems with this theory were that al-Zarqawi had barely worked under Osama bin Laden and had never worked with Saddam Hussein. There was no connection at all between al-Zarqawi and what happened on September 11, 2001. Regardless, the U.S. government was looking for a reason to send soldiers into Iraq to remove Saddam Hussein from power, and just like that, al-Zarqawi became the link to justify putting troops in Iraq.

HISTORY HAPPENED HERE: THE 9/11 MEMORIAL AND MUSEUM

On September 11, 2001, two of the four planes hijacked by al-Qaeda terrorists crashed into the Twin Towers of the World Trade Center in New York City. Thousands of people were killed on those planes and in those buildings, and to honor the lives lost that day, a memorial and museum were constructed on the site where the Twin Towers once stood.

The 9/11 Museum contains the most comprehensive collection of artifacts, personal accounts, and other displays and exhibits about the 9/11 attacks and those affected by them. The memorial features a plaza filled with trees, including the Survivor Tree, which was saved from the wreckage of the attacks. The centerpiece of the memorial is a pair of reflecting pools—waterfalls that pour down into the footprints of the Twin Towers. Around the pools are the names of those who were killed on 9/11, as well as those who were killed in the 1993 bombing of the World Trade Center, which was also carried out by al-Qaeda.

The 9/11 Memorial officially opened on September 11, 2011, the 10th anniversary of the attacks. People from around the world come to this site to honor the dead and remember this tragedy.

People who visit the 9/11 Memorial in New York City sometimes leave flowers near the name of a loved one who died that day.

In February 2003, Colin Powell, the U.S. secretary of state at the time, gave a speech to the United Nations (UN) describing the Iraqi weapons program headed by Saddam Hussein. The extent of this weapons program and the amount of danger it actually posed

Colin Powell is shown here addressing the United Nations on February 5, 2003. This speech is generally seen as the moment al-Zarqawi truly began to rise in power and prominence as a militant leader.

are still debated. In addition, CIA analysts warned against making direct connections between al-Zarqawi and the presence of al-Qaeda in Iraq. Regardless, this speech directly mentioned al-Zarqawi many times and named him as the link between al-Qaeda in Afghanistan and those weapons in Iraq. This relatively minor militant leader who had been turned away by al-Qaeda was suddenly world famous and began attracting more followers. Powell has since stated that he should have double-checked the facts of this speech, and he considers it a permanent stain on his record.

An Uprising Begins

The United States publicly disbanded Iraq's military in 2003. The former soldiers were unhappy with their sudden unemployment. They began to protest, and violence eventually broke out. Al-Zarqawi took advantage of this situation to recruit Muslims with combat training to his extremist cause. This marked the beginning of al-Zarqawi using suicide bombers to cause destruction, confusion, and fear in Iraq. By August 2003, his group—Jama'at al-Tawhid wa'al-Jihad (the Group of Monotheism and Jihad)—had bombed the UN headquarters in Baghdad, Iraq, and was the prime suspect in the bombing of the Jordanian embassy in that city as well. In those two attacks alone, more than 30 people were killed and at least 65 were wounded.

His group also bombed the mosque of Imam Ali, one of Iraq's holiest Shia shrines, killing more than 80 civilians while they prayed. Al-Zarqawi saw the Shia as servants of evil who would fight against the Sunni Muslims at the time of the apocalypse. He believed that putting any man-made law above the laws made by Allah was punishable by death, and he believed that the Shia did exactly this, which meant that as many as 200 million Muslims deserved to die in his eyes.

These attacks grabbed the attention of the United States. The CIA quickly released a statement to the president that said al-Zarqawi was leading an organized uprising.

FROM THE SOURCE: COLIN POWELL'S SPEECH TO THE UN

The following are excerpts from Colin Powell's February 2003 speech to the UN, in which he directly connected al-Zarqawi, al-Qaeda, and Saddam Hussein:

But what I want to bring to your attention today is the potentially much more sinister nexus between Iraq and the al-Qaida [al-Qaeda] terrorist network, a nexus that combines classic terrorist organizations and modern methods of murder. Iraq today harbors a deadly terrorist network headed by Abu Musab al-Zarqawi an associate and collaborator of Usama [Osama] bin Laden and his al-Qaida lieutenants …

When our coalition ousted the Taliban, the Zarqawi network helped establish another poison and explosive training center camp, and this camp is located in northeastern Iraq …

Zarqawi's activities are not confined to this small corner of northeast Iraq. He traveled to Baghdad in May of 2002 for medical treatment, staying in the capital of Iraq for two months while he recuperated to fight another day.

During his stay, nearly two dozen extremists converged on Baghdad and established a base of operations there. These al-Qaida affiliates based in Baghdad now coordinate the movement of people, money and supplies into and throughout Iraq for his network, and they have now been operating freely in the capital for more than eight months …

We are not surprised that Iraq is harboring Zarqawi and his subordinates. This understanding builds on decades-long experience with respect to ties between Iraq and al-Qaida.[1]

1. Secretary Colin L. Powell, "Remarks to the United Nations Security Council," U.S. Department of State Archive, February 5, 2003, 2001-2009.state.gov/secretary/former/powell/remarks/2003/17300.htm.

The CIA's claims were then supported by al-Zarqawi himself. In one of the most brutal messages of the Iraq War, he personally beheaded a prisoner and posted the video online. The man al-Zarqawi killed was an American freelance radio tower repairman named Nicholas Berg.

The U.S. government reacted by declaring a $25 million bounty on al-Zarqawi's head—the same price offered for bin Laden at the time. Al-Zarqawi was branded one of America's greatest enemies and was well on his way to earning his nickname: the Sheikh (king) of the Slaughterers.

The Beginning of AQI

Although the United States had portrayed al-Zarqawi as the link between al-Qaeda and Iraq in early 2003, it wasn't until late 2004 that al-Zarqawi formally agreed to join al-Qaeda and bin Laden formally agreed to accept him as part of the organization. Al-Zarqawi was motivated by the extra power that would come with being associated with al-Qaeda, and bin Laden believed this would give his organization a stronger presence in Iraq—and keep al-Zarqawi under his control. Al-Zarqawi took the title Emir (prince) of al-Qaeda's Operations in the Land of the Two Rivers (Iraq, through which both the Tigris and Euphrates Rivers flow). This was the beginning of al-Qaeda in Iraq, or AQI. However, bin Laden quickly saw how different al-Zarqawi's approach to terrorism was from his own.

Al-Qaeda aimed to unite Muslims against the West, but al-Zarqawi continued to murder Shia by the hundreds. When al-Zarqawi blew up the Shia mosque and attracted the support of Sunnis in Iraq, a civil war was sparked that ultimately killed tens of thousands of people. Al-Zarqawi counted on the Sunnis to resent the Shia, and with his encouragement, they did. He sent dozens of Sunni suicide bombers to blow up mosques, schools, and markets in Shia neighborhoods.

Al-Qaeda's senior leadership was sure the general Muslim public would reject al-Zarqawi's actions and believed that he would burn himself out and destroy his own vision through his enthusiasm for violence and his calls for civil war among Muslims. He was told he must consult with al-Qaeda before making any strategic decisions.

By 2006, though, al-Zarqawi saw himself as a commander and spiritual leader for Sunni Muslims across the globe. He now had influence over people, and as the leader of AQI, he had real power over Iraqi citizens. He demanded that all people follow his interpretation of sharia law: All women would wear veils, and all criminals would be beheaded. Even prominent figures in the community were publicly executed if they showed any resistance to al-Zarqawi's rule. Public beheadings were a major part of his reign of terror—a way to show his power to his enemies and to potential recruits.

PAST MEETS PRESENT: THE IRAQ WAR DEBATE

In March 2003, the United States invaded Iraq, and what's become known as the Iraq War began. From the beginning, there was always a contingent of Americans who opposed the war and believed that American troops were being sent in under false pretenses, especially concerning supposed weapons of mass destruction (WMD)—the chemical, biological, and nuclear weapons U.S. officials stated Saddam Hussein was hiding—and the links between al-Qaeda and the Iraqi leader. However, according to the Pew Research Center, 71 percent of Americans supported the decision to go to war in the days immediately following the invasion.

Over time, however, evidence emerged that there were no hidden WMD in Iraq and that there was no definitive link between Iraq and the 9/11 terrorist attacks. As this information came to light and more American lives were lost in Iraq, public opinion began to turn against the war. Large protests were held, and politicians who initially voted for and supported the war were often criticized by the American people.

The rise of ISIS in Iraq further turned public opinion against the war. Some Americans saw the 2003 invasion as an event that destabilized the region and allowed ISIS to gain power and followers. In 2018, a Pew Research Center poll found that 48 percent of Americans believed the use of force in Iraq in 2003 was the wrong decision, which was more than the 43 percent who believed it was the correct course of action.

Al-Zarqawi's period of militant leadership in Iraq did not last long, however. On June 7, 2006, U.S. forces dropped a pair of huge bombs on al-Zarqawi's hideout in the Iraqi village of Hibhib. Al-Qaeda in Iraq's leader, the Sheikh of the Slaughterers who had murdered hundreds of innocents, was killed in the aftermath. Any hopes of this being the end of AQI, though, were ultimately dashed. A new leader soon emerged, and AQI was on the verge of growing into the global terrorist threat known today as ISIS.

THEY MADE HISTORY: PRESIDENT GEORGE W. BUSH

George W. Bush was the president of the United States at the time of the 9/11 terrorist attacks, and he oversaw military actions in both Afghanistan and Iraq as part of what became known as the "War on Terror." His administration made many controversial decisions in the name of national security, but he was also praised by many Americans at the time for his empathetic leadership immediately after the most deadly terrorist attack on U.S. soil.

Bush was born on July 6, 1946, and his father, George H. W. Bush, served as president of the United States from 1989 to 1993. George W. Bush followed in his father's political footsteps after working in the oil and gas industry and investing in a Major League Baseball team (the Texas Rangers). In 1994, he was elected governor of Texas, and in 2000, he ran against Al Gore for U.S. president. While Gore ultimately won the popular vote in a close election that involved recounts in some places, Bush won the most votes in the Electoral College. He was sworn in as president in January 2001, less than a year before the attacks of September 11, 2001, occurred.

After leaving office in 2009, Bush and his wife, Laura, returned to Texas. In 2010, Bush published his presidential memoir, titled *Decision Points*. He's also become known for his paintings.

How You See History

1. Why do you think both Osama bin Laden and Abu Musab al-Zarqawi became Islamist extremists, despite having very different backgrounds?
2. Do you think naming al-Zarqawi as a link between al-Qaeda and Iraq was the right decision by U.S. leaders at the time? Why or why not?
3. Name some of the arguments for and against the Iraq War. Which side do you think makes a stronger case?

CHAPTER TWO

FROM AQI TO ISI

After Abu Musab al-Zarqawi's death in 2006, some people believed AQI would eventually fade from the international stage. Many people—including many Americans—saw Osama bin Laden and al-Qaeda as a far bigger threat than its Iraqi offshoot. With the terrorist attacks of September 11, 2001, still fresh in the minds of many, it was hard to imagine another terrorist group being able to spread the kind of fear and violence that al-Qaeda had spread in the 1990s and early 2000s.

While many remained focused on bin Laden and the original organization he founded, AQI continued to build a strong base of recruits and followers in Iraq. Although the group's first leader was dead, a new one took his place, and its violent attacks continued under a new name. It wouldn't be long before the violence it was causing in Iraq spread to many other parts of the world.

The Anbar Awakening

After al-Zarqawi's hideout was bombed by the United States, many Sunni groups began to revolt against AQI. Although they shared the same general religious beliefs as AQI, they didn't support the group's

AQI often used improvised explosive devices (IEDs) in its attacks, and ISIS has continued to use IED attacks to spread fear. Shown here is the aftermath of an explosion from a vehicle-borne improvised explosive device (VBIED). IEDs take the form of common objects and can injure or kill many people while not costing a lot of money to produce.

HISTORY HAPPENED HERE: IRAQ

Iraq has been an important part of the world since ancient times. It was known as Mesopotamia and was a cradle of early civilizations. Nestled between the Tigris and Euphrates Rivers, this land made up much of what is known as the Fertile Crescent—good land that allowed early peoples to farm and cultures to develop.

Over time, various empires attempted to control this fertile land and its people. It eventually became a central part of the Islamic world and was controlled by the Ottoman Empire, which was based in Turkey, until the end of World War I in 1918. Following the war, Iraq was controlled by Great Britain but became independent in 1932. The government in Iraq was generally unstable for many years, giving way to the rise of the Islamic nationalist Baath Party.

In 1979, Saddam Hussein took over as president of Iraq, but he was not the kind of president Americans are used to. He ruled as a dictator, committing many crimes against his own people and sending his nation into wars against Iran and later the United States and its allies. The Persian Gulf War (also known as the Gulf War or the First Gulf War) between Iraq and a group of nations led by the United States took place in 1991

methods. This was especially true in Anbar Province, which was a part of Iraq that had seen much violence and oppression from AQI.

The U.S. military saw this as an opportunity. General David Petraeus organized a revolt against AQI that was funded by the United States and became known as the Awakening. Any Sunnis who were willing to fight against AQI, even if they had previously fought against the Americans, were recruited for this effort and called the Sons of Iraq. This nickname was meant to unite the individual groups and to bring attention to the fact that most of AQI's leaders

as a retaliation against Iraq for invading its neighbor Kuwait in 1990. Various other international military operations took place in Iraq after 1991, including an operation in 1998 to destroy sites that were created to produce WMD.

The names of cities in Iraq are sometimes spelled differently in different sources.

In 2003, a coalition of nations, led once again by the United States, invaded Iraq and ousted Saddam Hussein from power. In 2006, the former leader of Iraq was executed for his crimes against humanity.

Iraq remains a nation struggling with political and social instability, which has made it a prime location for the growth of ISIS.

were foreigners, such as al-Zarqawi, who was from Jordan. These Sunnis believed that joining forces with the United States would spare them from punishment for previous crimes they had committed as part of Saddam Hussein's military.

The United States came to Iraq with the intention of bringing stability to the country and its people. However, Iraq did not necessarily embrace a foreign force attempting to control its territory, and violence continued in the country for many years after the Americans' arrival. The Awakening was designed to stop some of the

Shown here is General David Petraeus, who was the commander of coalition forces in Iraq during the time known as the Awakening. The coalition forces were made up of troops from the United States and a number of U.S. allies, including the United Kingdom.

violence still taking place in Iraq so the United States could withdraw its troops. It was not designed to repair the hatred between the Shia and the Sunnis that al-Zarqawi had encouraged. This responsibility was left to Iraq's new Shia government and Prime Minister Nouri al-Maliki.

Al-Maliki, however, failed to keep the peace. The Sons of Iraq did not trust him to provide the salaries or the government contracts they were promised, and he was accused of being biased against Sunnis and in favor of fellow Shia Muslims in his political and military appointments. His rule aggravated the wounds of division between Sunni and Shia Muslims, which allowed Islamist extremists to prey on the feelings of disillusionment felt by many Sunnis.

A Name Change

Despite the death of al-Zarqawi and the resistance from certain Iraqi groups, AQI had not totally disappeared. Not long after al-Zarqawi's death in 2006, his successor tried to bring the extremists back together. This man was known as Abu Ayyub al-Masri (and also as Abu Hamza al-Muhajir). Al-Masri was an Egyptian who, in 1982, joined the Egyptian Islamic Jihad in his home country. This organization was run by Osama bin Laden's future associate, Ayman al-Zawahiri. During the time al-Masri spent in this organization, he became an explosives expert. In Iraq, he recruited suicide bombers for AQI and personally carried out executions. He was relatively

THEY MADE HISTORY: GENERAL DAVID PETRAEUS

General David Petraeus has served his country in many different roles, but he later became infamous for a scandal that led to his resignation. He was born on November 7, 1952, in New York and attended the U.S. Military Academy at West Point before getting a doctoral degree in international relations from Princeton University.

In 2003, he led the 101st Airborne Division during the invasion of Iraq. He was then given the task of leading the training of Iraqi forces to take over control as the United States began to withdraw troops. Four years later, as the fighting in Iraq continued, Petraeus was named commander of the multinational forces—led by the United States—in the country. The next year, he was appointed head of Centcom (Central Command), controlling all U.S. military operations in an area stretching from Africa to Central Asia. In 2010, Petraeus was named the commander of all forces in Afghanistan.

The next phase of Petraeus's career began in 2011, when President Barack Obama nominated him to lead the CIA. He was unanimously confirmed by the Senate and retired from the U.S. Army that year. However, in 2012, he resigned from his position and revealed that he'd had an affair with the woman who was writing his biography. In 2015, he pled guilty to sharing classified information with her, but because the information was never published or released to the public, he was fined but not sent to jail.

unknown on the international stage at the time he was chosen to succeed al-Zarqawi, but his selection was not a total surprise to U.S. intelligence organizations, who believed he was a credible choice to take over AQI.

Al-Masri is most famous for renaming AQI the Islamic State of Iraq, or ISI, which is also sometimes known as the Islamic

State in Iraq. This group also included members of other Iraqi Islamist groups who joined together for a common extremist cause. The Islamic State of Iraq chose its new name purposefully. It was chosen not only to unite various Iraqi extremist groups but also to highlight the group's true goal: the establishment of one Islamic state, or *dawla*. The idea of creating a caliphate that would extend sharia law through violence was reflected in this new name.

The change of name confused the supporters of al-Qaeda. Was the Islamic State of Iraq trying to break away from AQI? The decision to change the name was done reportedly without consulting Osama bin Laden. This weakened ties between ISI and al-Qaeda and caused growing tension between its leaders.

Organizing ISI

One of al-Masri's first public moves was to definitively declare that the terrorist organization would continue to fight Shia Muslims and Western troops. He also appointed a new person to lead his newly named organization—an Iraqi extremist to lead an Iraqi Islamist group.

Al-Masri knew there needed to be a commander of the faithful for the new Islamic State of Iraq. His first step was to find the perfect man for the role. He eventually decided on Abu Omar al-Baghdadi, who was originally known as Hamid al-Zawi, a former police officer from a small farming town in Iraq. He was fired from the police force in the early 1990s for his extremely conservative religious views. He lived a relatively simple life in Baghdad until the Americans invaded Iraq in 2003. He then led Iraqi fighters against the American troops. He also took the name Abu Omar al-Baghdadi in an attempt to emphasize that he lived in Baghdad. His appointment to leader of the organization seemed to be based on very little. It was also confusing because al-Qaeda's members had pledged allegiance to Mullah Omar, who had been named commander of the faithful by the Taliban. Some even doubted that Abu Omar al-Baghdadi was a real person.

Al-Masri gave Abu Omar al-Baghdadi this position because the Islamic State needed to be structured like a real government, and the commander of the faithful was its head. It was helpful to have an Iraqi as the head of ISI. However, Abu Omar al-Baghdadi was easy to manipulate. Al-Masri was the real person in power.

Al-Qaeda leaders began to worry that the Islamic State of Iraq was going to distance itself from their rule, especially after it changed its name and pledged allegiance to a new ruler who had not been approved by Osama bin Laden. In addition, ISI began to distance itself further through the creation of a governing structure for the Islamic State. Al-Masri named himself the minister of war in the Islamic State's first cabinet and began to formally organize its terrorists into a military.

All of these moves helped identify al-Masri as someone who had big-picture politics in mind. Rather than just focusing on the brutal violence that al-Zarqawi popularized, he wanted to build the new Islamic world. His eventual plan was to expand the Islamic State into a global caliphate, although he still planned to do this using extremist violence. Some modern observers have pointed this out as the major difference between al-Masri and al-Zarqawi. Both men were incredibly dangerous and willing to murder as many people as they needed to, but al-Zarqawi did not have any real plans to establish his caliphate. Al-Masri was always working toward this end goal.

Many Islamist extremists were critical of this new leadership. Some said that the Islamic State had no land, so it failed to meet the requirements of a real state. Many Sunni groups protested because they only wanted to liberate Iraq, not create an Islamic state. Additionally, ISI had challenged the authority of bin Laden and al-Qaeda. Many of ISI's fighters, though, were loyal to bin Laden and his organization.

Although it was not happy with the defiance of ISI, al-Qaeda publicly endorsed the establishment of the Islamic State. Osama bin Laden's trusted advisor, al-Zawahiri, stated in December 2007:

> *I want to clarify that there is nothing in Iraq by the name of al Qaeda. Rather, the organization of [AQI] merged, by the grace of God, with other jihadi groups in the Islamic State of Iraq,*

may God protect it. It is a legitimate emirate established on a legitimate and sound method. It was established through consultation and won the oath of allegiance from most of the mujahids [fighters] and tribes in Iraq.[1]

Struggles Under al-Masri

Al-Masri attempted to unite Muslims under a single black flag representing the Islamic State. However, he was not a successful leader. In 2006, at the beginning of his Islamic State career, the U.S. government offered a $5 million bounty for information about his location; by 2008, they were offering only $100,000. Al-Masri often did not know what his subordinates were doing, and he was very far removed from the reality of ISI's actions.

Sunnis who tried to resist ISI were told they could either join or hand over their weapons. ISI members began kidnapping and executing those who resisted to demonstrate their power over Iraqi citizens. Another radical group, named the Islamic Army in Iraq, refused to bow to ISI, and violent fighting broke out between the two groups. Some reports have stated that members of the Islamic Army later teamed up with U.S. troops to push back against ISI.

Al-Masri continued to demonstrate his inability to manage the Islamic State. Complaints were written to al-Qaeda in Afghanistan concerning the division in Iraq, and ISI's violence toward other Iraqi groups made it easier for Americans to recruit Iraqis to the cause of weakening ISI.

ISI in Decline

In August 2007, a man named Abu Sulayman al-Utaybi was removed from his position as the chief sharia law judge of the Islamic State of Iraq because of disagreements with al-Masri. Shortly afterward, he approached al-Qaeda to accuse al-Masri of running the Islamic State of Iraq poorly. The leaders of al-Qaeda were worried that al-Masri was not a strong leader and was appointing the wrong people to help him run ISI. There was also uncertainty surrounding what would happen if al-Masri were to die, which was dangerous because a clear chain of command was important to keep ISI going.

PAST MEETS PRESENT: THE MAHDI AND THE APOCALYPSE

The apocalypse, or the end of the world, is an important idea for the Islamic State, as it is for many fundamental branches of a variety of religions, including Christianity. In Christianity, Jesus Christ is seen as the savior and redeemer who will appear at the end of the world to restore justice. The Islamic State and other Muslim groups believe in a similar figure known as the Mahdi.

The first man who used the Mahdi as a political tool was Al-Mukhtar ibn Abu Ubayd al-Thaqafi. Born in the seventh century, he led a revolutionary rebellion against the Umayyad caliphate in Iraq. He taught his followers that they needed to overthrow the government to prepare the world for the Mahdi.

This savior figure was important for many Muslims because he would supposedly signal that the apocalypse was near. He was described as being the leader of Islam's armies in the world's final battle. The prophecies about the Mahdi were not found in the Quran but in volumes called *hadith*. These were written many years after the Prophet Muhammad's death but were believed to contain his teachings and sayings.

Over the centuries, some men have claimed to be the Mahdi, just as some men have claimed to be Jesus Christ or another figure meant to herald the coming apocalypse. In the 21st century, the Islamic State has taken advantage of the ideas of the Mahdi to proclaim that they are fighting a good fight that will hasten his arrival and the time of the final judgment, when those who follow their ways will be rewarded. They bring up the apocalypse and the Mahdi as a way of controlling their followers and recruiting more. Similar tactics have been used by other religious groups throughout history, as well as non-religious "doomsday cults" made up of people who are awaiting or who have predicted the end of the world.

FROM THE SOURCE: "THE SOLE FLAG FOR ALL MUSLIMS"

In an effort to prove its legitimate statehood, shortly after being established, the Islamic State revealed its flag. It is black with white letters stating, in Arabic, "There is only one God, Allah," and underneath that, it features a white circle with black lettering that reads, "Muhammad is his messenger." The Islamic State and its followers believe this is the flag that all Muslims should follow when the end of the world comes.

When the flag was first introduced, the Islamic State concluded its description with the following prayer: "We ask God, praised be He, to make this flag the sole flag for all Muslims. We are certain that it will be the flag of the people of Iraq when they go to aid … the Mahdi at the holy house of God."[1]

1.Quoted in William McCants, "How ISIS Got Its Flag," *Atlantic*, September 22, 2015, www.theatlantic.com/international/archive/2015/09/isis-flag-apocalypse/406498/.

Shown here is the flag of the Islamic State. Its black color symbolizes vengeance, or violent punishment for an injury or offense.

Al-Masri was called upon in letters to answer to al-Qaeda's leaders. Meanwhile, his accuser, al-Utaybi, was killed by U.S. forces.

It was a bad time for the cause of the Islamic State, which was good for the rest of Iraq. In early 2007, roughly 2,500 civilians were killed each month. By the end of 2008, this number had been reduced to 500 per month. Although these deaths were still tragic, Iraq's Sunni tribes were starting to contain the Islamic State of Iraq while the United States got rid of its leadership. This damaged ISI's reputation: Potential recruits had trouble believing that the Islamic State had Allah's support if it was being defeated by outsiders.

Many still referred to ISI as al-Qaeda in Iraq, so this bad reputation reflected on the original al-Qaeda in Afghanistan. However, bin Laden still refused to formally denounce the Islamic State of Iraq.

A joint American-Iraqi raid in April 2010 brought about the deaths of both Abu Ayyub al-Masri and Abu Omar al-Baghdadi. Shortly after their deaths, a man named Abu Bakr al-Baghdadi was appointed as ISI's new commander of the faithful. Just as with Abu Omar al-Baghdadi, few had ever heard of him. However, he would soon become known around the world as the leader of ISIS.

How You See History

1. Why do you think Sunnis who originally fought against the United States were willing to join the Awakening?
2. Can you think of other groups besides the Islamic State that have used a figure like the Mahdi to call for violence against people who don't share their beliefs?
3. What were some of the main causes of tension between ISI and al-Qaeda? Why do you think Osama bin Landen refused to publicly cut ties with ISI?

BAGH

CHAPTER THREE

A NEW LEADER

Between 2006 and 2010, the Islamic State was seemingly in a period of decline marked by leadership failures, American and Iraqi intervention, and power struggles with al-Qaeda. However, this difficult time for the terrorist organization was not the beginning of its end, as many hoped. Instead, it was a period of transition, and in 2010, the Islamic State began to find its footing again under the leadership of a new commander of the faithful: Abu Bakr al-Baghdadi. He would come to be known as a far more successful leader than any of his predecessors, although his success at leading and expanding the Islamic State was anything but positive, resulting in large-scale death and destruction around the world.

To better understand the growth of the Islamic State, it's important to take a close look at the man who led it during the peak of its reign of terror. His journey from middle-class Muslim to the world's most-wanted terrorist provides important information about the recruitment, training, and psychology of those who resort to extremist violence.

A Student of the Quran

Ibrahim Awad Ibrahim Ali al-Badri (al-Samarrai is sometimes added to the end) was 39 years old when he assumed the name Abu Bakr al-Baghdadi and the Islamic State position of commander of the faithful.

Although Abu Bakr al-Baghdadi recruited many Muslims to fight for the Islamic State, many more strongly protested his violent actions, including the members of India's Shia community, who staged the demonstration shown here, which included burning photos of the ISIS leader.

He was born in 1971 to a lower–middle class Sunni farming family and grew up in Samarra, Iraq. His father taught about the Quran in the local mosque and was a religious man. Al-Badri was proud of his lineage, claiming to be a descendant of the Prophet Muhammad, which helped add credibility to his leadership of the Islamic State later in his life.

Al-Badri was quiet and devout as a young person. In fact, his nickname while growing up was "the Believer." When he was not at school or playing soccer, he was at the local mosque. He taught younger members of the community about the Quran when he was a teenager. He was also a gifted speaker who excelled at memorizing the Quran and reading its verses to others. Even among friends and family, he was quick to scold anyone who did not strictly follow Islamic law. Al-Badri wanted to study law at the University of Baghdad, but because his high school grades were not good enough, he studied the Quran instead.

After his undergraduate education, al-Badri enrolled in Saddam University, where he obtained his master's degree in 1999 and his doctorate in topics related to the study of the Quran. During graduate school, his uncle, Ismail al-Badri, convinced him to join the Muslim Brotherhood. The goal of the Muslim Brotherhood was to establish Islamic governments. Most branches of the Brotherhood were peaceful. Some members were liberal, and others were conservative. The young al-Badri eventually gravitated toward the more extreme corners of the Brotherhood.

Between 2000 and 2004, not much is known about al-Badri's activities. Some reports have stated that he had two wives and six children, but much conflicting information has been released about his personal life. He and his growing family did not socialize much. He taught recitation, or reading, of the Quran at the neighborhood mosque and led the call to prayer. He also continued to play soccer and coached younger players, whom he tried to instruct in the ways of conservative Islam. He was known for losing his temper whenever he saw behavior that he thought went against the teachings of the Quran. This obsession with maintaining a strict Muslim code would foreshadow his leadership of the Islamic State.

Another Kind of University

After the Americans overpowered Saddam Hussein's army in 2003, al-Badri helped develop a rebel group that fought the U.S. troops and their

Some people believe Camp Bucca (*shown here*) is where al-Badri was radicalized, or inspired to become a radical Islamist extremist. However, other sources have reported that he was already exhibiting violent extremist views before his imprisonment.

allies in Iraq. This group was called Jaysh Ahl al-Sunna wa-l-Jamaah, or the Army of the People of the Sunna and Communal Solidarity.

In early 2004, al-Badri was arrested by the U.S. military in Fallujah, Iraq, for being associated with Islamist extremists. He was held for nearly a year at the prison Camp Bucca as a civilian detainee. This meant that the Americans did not officially associate him with a terrorist group. His jailers did not know he was a militant Islamist.

Much like al-Zarqawi before him, al-Badri was shaped by his time in prison. He stayed serious, led prayers, and conducted religious classes. He even had the opportunity to impress everyone on the soccer field. Although he was quiet, he had a natural air of authority and leadership around him. One of his fellow prisoners explained, "He has a charisma. You could feel that he was someone important."[1]

The United States did not know it, but Camp Bucca became a cultivation center for extremist beliefs and plans. Many inmates were Sunnis who had served Saddam Hussein, and the conditions were perfect for them to be exposed to—and adopt—militant Islamist beliefs. According to a report by William McCants for the research group the Brookings Institution:

> *"New recruits were prepared so that when they were freed they were ticking time bombs," remembers [a] fellow inmate [of al-Badri's], who was interviewed by a reporter with* Al Monitor. *When a new prisoner came in, his peers would "teach him, indoctrinate him, and give him direction so he leaves a burning flame."*[2]

Prisons such as Camp Bucca became known as "jihadi universities" because they held a large number of people with similar Islamist interests who were creating networks and learning to become terrorists. In fact, the inmate who described al-Badri's charisma added, "If there was no American prison in Iraq, there would be no [Islamic State] now."[3] For

HISTORY HAPPENED HERE: FALLUJAH

Not long after al-Badri was arrested in Fallujah, Iraq, the city became a major focal point of the conflict between U.S.-led coalition forces and Islamist fighters. Known as the "city of mosques" because of its many Islamic places of worship, Fallujah (also known by the name al-Falluja) didn't see much action during the initial U.S. invasion of Iraq in 2003. However, in 2004, unrest began to spread in the city. Protests that turned violent led to the deaths of Iraqi citizens, and American contractors were killed in an ambush. In response, the First Battle of Fallujah was fought in April and May 2004, but U.S. air strikes led to so much destruction and death that the Iraqis pressured the United States to fall back. Although Iraqi troops were supposed to hold down the city, it eventually fell to the insurgents—those who fought against the United States and the new Iraqi government.

With insurgents, including members of AQI, in control of the city, the Americans mounted an offensive to take it back in late 2004. During the Second Battle of Fallujah, fierce urban warfare led to even more destruction and casualties, including the deaths of more than 100 coalition troops and an unknown number of civilians, which some estimates have placed in the thousands. Most of the population who survived were forced to flee. However, the insurgents were driven out, and people began to return to the city, though anti-American feelings remained.

Ten years after the battles that took place there, Fallujah was once again under siege, as ISIS forces took over. In 2016, Iraqi troops liberated the city from ISIS control, but the Iraqi civilian population in Fallujah once again suffered devastating losses.

al-Badri, his imprisonment provided a tremendous opportunity to make connections and friends with former members of Saddam Hussein's army—friends who would later happily join the Islamic State. They were able to reconnect after being released from prison because they had reportedly written one another's phone numbers in the elastic of their underwear.

FROM THE SOURCE: INSIDE CAMP BUCCA

As ISIS began to gain more power, journalists and others were tasked with investigating how this group rose so quickly. In one article for the *Washington Post*, multiple sources described how conditions inside Camp Bucca and other prison camps made it very easy for Islamist extremists to recruit fellow prisoners to their cause:

> *As news of Baghdadi's tenure at Bucca emerged, former prison commander James Skylar Gerrond remembered many of them. "Re: Badghadi," he wrote on Twitter in July [2014], "Many of us at Camp Bucca were concerned that instead of just holding detainees, we had created a pressure cooker for extremism … "*
>
> *"Sharia courts enforce a lot of rules inside the compounds," one soldier … said. "Anyone who takes part in behavior which is seen as 'Western' is severely punished by the extremist elements of the compound … It's quite appalling sometimes."*
>
> *Prison commanders such as Gerrond observed the growing extremism. "There was a huge amount of collective pressure exerted on detainees to become more radical in their beliefs," he told* Mother Jones. *"… Detainees turn[ed] to each other for support. If there were radical elements within this support network, there was always the potential that detainees would become more radical."*[1]

1. Terrence McCoy, "How the Islamic State Evolved in an American Prison," *Washington Post*, November 4, 2014, www.washingtonpost.com/news/morning-mix/wp/2014/11/04/how-an-american-prison-helped-ignite-the-islamic-state/.

Rise to Power

After he was released from prison, al-Badri was drawn to al-Qaeda's extremist views of Islam and became connected with its branch in Iraq. AQI sent him to Syria because it was easier for him to escape notice by the Americans there. His job was to make sure that all of AQI's online recruiting and information reflected its conservative interpretation of Islam. He was also able to help several foreign jihadists cross Syria's border into Iraq. After AQI became ISI, al-Badri continued to work for the organization, managing the religious affairs of the group in some parts of Iraq. In addition, Jaysh Ahl al-Sunna wa-l-Jamaah became one of the first Iraqi groups to join the new Islamic State.

By doing good work for ISI, al-Badri was building up his reputation among its top leaders. He quickly won over both Abu Omar al-Baghdadi and Abu Ayyub al-Masri because of his academic credentials and the work he had done supervising religious affairs. Al-Masri named al-Badri as the supervisor of the Sharia Committee, which was responsible for enforcing ISI's strict Islamic code. He was eventually named to the Consultative Council, a group of advisors who were supposed to assist Abu Omar al-Baghdadi but really worked for al-Masri. Al-Badri was now very close to the leaders of the Islamic State; he was trusted with their secrets and plans. He was responsible for coordinating communication between those leaders and would also sometimes communicate with their al-Qaeda bosses on their behalf.

When the top two leaders in the Islamic State were killed, al-Qaeda in Afghanistan cautioned ISI not to be too quick to appoint a new leader. Bin Laden told the Consultative Council to appoint a temporary leader and to send him a list of candidates and their credentials. Growing more and more independent, the Islamic State ignored him.

A man named Hajji Bakr was head of the Islamic State's military council at the time; this made him a powerful figure when Abu Ayyub al-Masri and Abu Omar al-Baghdadi were killed. Trying to control the succession of a new leader of ISI, he reportedly wrote to each of the members of the Consultative Council claiming that everyone had agreed that Ibrahim Awad Ibrahim al-Badri should be in charge. It is not completely clear why Bakr chose al-Badri, but al-Badri had quite a few things in his favor: He had been close to the previous leader, he had powerful friends, and above all,

Both Abu Omar al-Baghdadi and Abu Bakr al-Baghdadi were from Iraq, which is reflected in the "al-Baghdadi" parts of their names. This references the Iraqi capital of Baghdad, shown here.

THEY MADE HISTORY: ABU BAKR

Al-Badri's new name was not chosen at random. Abu Bakr was the name of the Prophet Muhammad's father-in-law. Like Muhammad, Abu Bakr was also born in Mecca in today's Saudi Arabia. He was very close to his son-in-law and advised him as Muhammad became a religious and political leader. Muhammad trusted him enough to call upon him to lead the faithful if he were to die.

After Muhammad's death in 632, Abu Bakr took his place and became the first caliph of the Islamic world. The title of "caliph" means "successor" in Arabic and is a reflection of the fact that Abu Bakr succeeded Muhammad as the leader of the Islamic community. He fought off various rebellions by different groups and expanded the reach of Islam. In addition, he began to send armies into the area known as the Levant, which contributed to the spread of Islam long after his death in 634.

he claimed descent from the Prophet Muhammad. Bakr believed that al-Badri could help the Islamic State make a major comeback.

These efforts by Hajji Bakr were successful—al-Badri became Abu Bakr al-Baghdadi, the third leader of Iraq's growing terrorist organization. All other leaders in the Islamic State who were suspected of disloyalty were dismissed. If they did not go willingly, Bakr had them killed. With any enemies or challengers to his authority removed from ISI, al-Baghdadi's power was absolute within the organization.

A Growing Power in Iraq

By the time al-Baghdadi took over control of the Islamic State in 2010, its power and influence had been weakened. It possessed no land, which was a problem for a group claiming to be a state. It blamed this misfortune on the Americans and the Sunni tribes who had been "awakened" by General Petraeus to fight against them. With al-Baghdadi in power, though, the Islamic State promised itself, its remaining followers, and its enemies that it would recover.

PAST MEETS PRESENT: RECRUITING TERRORISTS ONLINE

Islamist terrorist groups such as ISIS have been using the internet for many years to recruit people around the world to their cause. They are often held up as the most common example of the kinds of terrorists radicalized and recruited online. However, in recent years, a growing number of white nationalist terrorists have spread their messages of hatred and violence on the internet as well.

White nationalists believe that white people are inherently better than people of color and, therefore, should be the only people allowed to be part of a given nation, such as the United States. This kind of hateful message is spread on the internet, and some white nationalists—much like some Islamist extremists—have taken their hatred offline and committed acts of horrific violence. For example, in August 2019, a man shot and killed more than 20 people at a Walmart store in El Paso, Texas, because he wanted to murder members of the Hispanic community. He posted a white nationalist statement online before the shooting.

Social media platforms such as Twitter are sometimes seen as places for people to share their violent attitudes toward women, people of color, people of other religions, and people with different political beliefs under the protection of free speech. However, as that hatred has led to acts of terrorism, social media platforms are being asked to come up with new solutions to stop the spread of terrorist propaganda of all kinds.

The Islamic State wanted to instill fear in Iraq. It did this by developing a media strategy to show off its brutal methods to the public. Videos of the executions of those who resisted ISI's rule were taken and shared online. Victims included Iraqis and captured Westerners, including humanitarian aid workers.

In addition to spreading intimidation in Iraq and around the world, the Islamic State's carefully constructed media presence contributed to its recruitment. Thousands of foreign Muslims from all over the world, including France, the United Kingdom, Belgium,

Iraqi civilians have suffered greatly during the Islamic State's reign of terror in their country. From January 2014 to October 2015, the United Nations (UN) reported that more than 18,000 Iraqi civilians had been killed because of violence connected with the Islamic State. Many more had been injured, enslaved, or displaced from their homes, such as the Iraqi civilians shown here.

Germany, Holland, Australia, Indonesia, and the United States, traveled to join the ranks of ISI fighters. These men and women wanted to fight under al-Baghdadi and were more than willing to die for their beliefs. Many were radicalized online and were inspired by the power the Islamic State displayed through its brutal acts of terror. While groups of foreign Muslims traveled to the Middle East to fight for the Islamic State, other recruits carried out attacks influenced by the message of al-Baghdadi in other countries.

Under al-Baghdadi's influence, the Islamic State became stronger. Those who followed him believed he was a true caliph, descended from the Prophet Muhammad. Although most Muslims have renounced the Islamic State, those who have chosen to fight for it believe they are justified in their actions. They believe it's their calling to purify the world by killing those who stand in the way of the spread of Islam and the development of the caliphate.

As the Islamic State continued to grow in power and influence under al-Baghdadi, it also began to acquire the lands it needed to claim that it was a legitimate state ruled by a legitimate caliph. Through acts of deadly violence, it began to conquer territory in Iraq and also on a new front as well. Al-Baghdadi had his sights set on Syria, and once ISI took its campaign of brutal violence into that unstable nation, the Islamic State of Iraq officially became ISIS—the Islamic State in Iraq and Syria.

How You See History

1. Why do you think U.S. prisons in Iraq became "jihadi universities"?
2. Why do you think Hajji Bakr was so convinced that Abu Bakr al-Baghdadi was the right person to lead the Islamic State?
3. Should websites and social media platforms be doing more to stop terrorists from using the internet as a recruitment tool? Why or why not?

CHAPTER FOUR

CREATING THE CALIPHATE

Political, social, and economic instability has always been a driving force in the development of terrorist organizations. In the 1980s and beyond, instability in Afghanistan allowed al-Qaeda to form and gain power. Similarly, in the 2010s, a civil war in Syria created the kind of unstable conditions terrorist groups seize as opportunities to expand their reach. As Syria fell into chaos, Abu Bakr al-Baghdadi and his followers entered the scene, taking control of large parts of the country in an effort to establish a caliphate that spread beyond ISI's original reach.

Meanwhile, continued instability in Iraq allowed the Islamic State to capture and control major cities, including Mosul—the second largest city in Iraq. As al-Baghdadi increased his power and the lands under his control, he publicly took on the mantle of caliph and claimed the establishment of a caliphate centered in Iraq and Syria. By 2014, ISI had officially become ISIS and was ruling large parts of Iraq and Syria with an iron fist. However, not all of al-Baghdadi's former allies were pleased with his progress in establishing a caliphate. In fact, al-Qaeda officially cut ties with its former offshoot over the Islamic State's presence in Syria, creating a very public rift between the world's two most infamous terrorist organizations.

Shown here is damage from the fighting that took place in Mosul, Iraq, during its occupation by ISIS. Mosul was one of the most important cities held by the terrorist group during the height of its power.

Although many people in the United States and Europe are most familiar with the violent actions of ISIS followers against Western targets, it has caused the most death and destruction close to home. In his quest to establish a true caliphate and declare himself leader of the Muslim world, al-Baghdadi was prepared to eliminate anyone who stood in his way—from the U.S. military to fellow Muslims.

Unrest in Syria

According to U.S. intelligence reports, in 2007, nearly 90 percent of the foreign fighters who were arriving in Iraq to fight for the Islamic State were coming through Syria. The reason why ISIS and other terrorist groups have been able to recruit heavily through Syria is because of that country's recent history of political unrest and violence. Countries plagued with violence are much easier to use for extremist purposes, and the Syrian people's struggles with their government began in earnest with their former president, Hafiz al-Assad, in the 1980s.

Hafiz al-Assad rose to power in Syria during the 1960s and 1970s when his political party overthrew the government. After being elected president in 1971, he was quick to suppress anyone who spoke against his new government. In addition to arresting or killing political activists, Hafiz al-Assad's most infamous deed was putting down an uprising in the Syrian city of Hama, which was a stronghold of the Muslim Brotherhood, in 1982. Part of this military action resulted in the massacre of tens of thousands of civilians. (Estimates vary, but most human rights groups and historians place the total number of civilian casualties between 10,000 and 30,000.) Although this kind of brutal violence made al-Assad powerful, his son, who would become president of Syria in 2000, learned that his people would tolerate that kind of oppression for only a few more years.

When Bashar al-Assad succeeded his father as Syrian president, some people were optimistic that he would reform the tyrannical practices of the government. Bashar himself pledged to make his presidency less bloody and more open than his father's. For a few months after he assumed power, he kept these promises.

Bashar al-Assad (*shown here*) has been accused of using chemical weapons to attack his own people.

Soon, however, he began to crack down just as violently on political activists and anyone who spoke against his policies. Syrians endured this bad treatment for another decade.

Shortly after Abu Bakr al-Baghdadi took power over the Islamic State, Syrians began coming together to protest the government of Bashar al-Assad. The protests started after the arrests and torture of 15 students for painting antigovernment graffiti on the walls of a school. The community was outraged at how the children were treated. The citizens refused to be intimidated by the police and gathered in the streets to march and demonstrate against Assad.

As unrest turned into a civil war, Syrians began demanding that Assad give up his position. In response to these demands, Assad released hundreds of prisoners—many of them Islamist terrorists—in order to create violence among the protesters and have a seemingly just cause for a forceful crackdown. He has consistently claimed that Islamist terrorists are behind his country's civil war.

When Assad did this, the Islamic State deployed a group to Syria to take advantage of the chaos. Al-Baghdadi sent Abu Muhammad al-Jawlani (sometimes spelled al-Julani) to oversee this effort and establish a branch of the Islamic State in Syria. This new group called themselves Jabhat al-Nusra, or the al-Nusra Front.

HISTORY HAPPENED HERE: SYRIA

Syria has a long and complex history that stretches back to ancient times. Nestled between Iraq and the Mediterranean Sea, it was an important cradle of early civilizations in the Middle East. It was ruled by many different empires throughout ancient history, including the Assyrians, Babylonians, and Persians. Eventually, it fell under the control of Alexander the Great and later the Roman Empire.

The capital of Syria, Damascus, was an important place in the early centuries of Christianity and the Byzantine Empire. However, by the 630s CE, Muslim armies had laid claim to Syria and used Damascus as the capital of their growing Islamic empire. However, the capital eventually moved, and Syria was ruled by a number of different groups again before it was placed under the control of the Ottoman Empire from 1516 to 1918.

France was the reigning power in Syria following World War I, which ended in 1918. Although various rebellions and uprisings took place against French rule, no major changes were enacted until 1936, when Syria was granted

Separating Over Syria

The al-Nusra Front began as a small jihadist group in Syria, but it grew quickly, taking responsibility for numerous suicide bombings throughout the country. In its first videotaped statement, a masked spokesperson for the group talked about the attacks it had carried out and stated, "We are Syrian mujahideen, back from various jihad fronts to restore God's rule on the Earth and avenge the Syrians' violated honour and spilled blood." He continued, "Jabhat al-Nusra has taken upon itself to be the Muslim nation's weapon in this land."[1] Al-Nusra means "support" in Arabic, and the group gained a reputation for working with other Syrian rebels in cities such as Aleppo.

some independence, although it still had to defer to France on matters such as economic and foreign policy. After World War II ended in 1945, Syria was ruled jointly by Great Britain and France, but by 1946, troops from those countries had officially withdrawn from Syria. The country finally saw itself as fully independent. Only a little more than a decade after that, though, Hafiz al-Assad rose to power, and this nation, which had been plagued by instability throughout history, was the site of unrest once again.

Like cities in Iraq, Syrian cities often have many variations in their spellings from one source to another. These cities have often been plagued by instability and violence throughout history.

As the al-Nusra Front began to gain more recognition and influence in Syria, Abu Bakr al-Baghdadi looked to join forces with al-Jawlani and bring the al-Nusra Front officially under the umbrella of the Islamic State. Al-Jawlani refused. Despite al-Jawlani's resistance, al-Baghdadi took the initiative in April 2013 to claim the al-Nusra Front as part of the Islamic State. He declared that the al-Nusra Front would be absorbed into a new organization: the Islamic State in Iraq and Syria—ISIS.

Al-Jawlani wasn't going to accept al-Baghdadi's bullying. He declared independence from the Islamic State and publicly pledged allegiance to al-Qaeda and Ayman al-Zawahiri, its leader following the death of Osama bin Laden. In response, al-Qaeda scolded both

PAST MEETS PRESENT: THE SYRIAN REFUGEE CRISIS

The civil war in Syria has forced many civilians to leave their homes and their entire lives behind. Within Syria, more than 6 million people have been displaced, which means they've had to move to another part of the country because of the war. In addition, more than 5 million Syrians have become refugees who have been forced to leave their home country and seek protection in another country. At least half of all Syrian refugees are under the age of 18. According to Filippo Grandi, the High Commissioner of the UNHCR, which is the part of the United Nations that deals with helping refugees, "Syria is the biggest humanitarian and refugee crisis of our time."[1]

Many Syrian refugees have settled in Turkey and other neighboring countries, but others have made the difficult journey to Europe and the United States. In some cases, they've been welcomed. In other cases, though, people have treated them with suspicion or even outright hostility because they're afraid that Syrian refugees might actually be Islamist terrorists due to the presence of ISIS in the country.

Americans have been sharply divided about helping Syrian refugees. According to a 2017 poll by the Pew Research Center, 47 percent of Americans believe the United States has a responsibility to take in Syrian refugees, but 48 percent believe the United States doesn't have a responsibility to do so.

1. Quoted in "Syria Emergency," UNHCR, www.unhcr.org/en-us/syria-emergency.html (accessed May 20, 2020).

men and told the Islamic State to stay within Iraq while the al-Nusra Front would continue to fight in Syria under al-Qaeda. Al-Baghdadi rejected this decision and continued operating in Syria, eventually engaging in violent clashes with the al-Nusra Front. In early 2014, al-Qaeda publicly renounced any connection to the Islamic State.

The relations between the two terrorist organizations were poor. Abu Khalid al-Suri, the man chosen by al-Qaeda to help the situation between the al-Nusra Front and the Islamic State, was disgusted. He said, "The State group is excommunicating everyone who opposes them or differs with them, spilling their blood with [no punishment] as if they own Islam."[2] In response, the Islamic State threatened to send suicide bombers to murder him; later, it followed through with that threat.

In 2016, the al-Nusra Front was renamed Jabhat Fateh al-Sham and cut ties with al-Qaeda. The next year, it merged with several other groups in Syria to form Hay'at Tahrir al-Sham.

The Fall of Mosul

Al-Baghdadi entered Syria and quickly set up the ISIS headquarters in the northern city of Raqqa. With the leader of ISIS gone from Iraq, the Iraqi government started to crack down on the Sunni population. Prime Minister Nouri al-Maliki took the opportunity of al-Baghdadi's absence to try to suppress any resistance by the Sunnis. Near the start of 2014, al-Baghdadi turned his attention back to his home country, beginning with the capture of Fallujah in January.

Many oppressed Sunnis were eager to join ISIS—not necessarily because they were violent extremists, but because they wanted to end what they saw as the tyranny of al-Maliki. These new recruits allowed ISIS to keep a strong presence in Syria while simultaneously conquering Iraqi cities. Their most important capture was the city of Mosul, Iraq's second-largest population center. ISIS fighters overwhelmed the city, causing Iraqi government soldiers and police officers to abandon their posts while thousands of Iraqi civilians fled. The fall of Mosul on June 10, 2014, greatly exposed the weakness of Iraq's security forces, and ISIS was able to capture an arsenal of weapons and military equipment.

Mosul was a significant win for al-Baghdadi. It is located in a strategically important intersection, linking Iraq to Turkey and Syria. Prime Minister al-Maliki declared a state of emergency and

FROM THE SOURCE: A CIVILIAN'S ACCOUNT OF LIFE IN RAQQA

ISIS controlled Raqqa for more than three years, and during that time, life was very difficult for civilians living in the capital of the Islamic State. The following is part of an account of life in Raqqa told to the British newspaper *The Guardian* in 2017 by a Syrian journalist using the pen name Tim Ramadan:

> *Nobody likes living under Isis's control, being forced to follow their laws and exposed to danger on a daily basis. We lead double lives as a condition of our survival. Everyone has at least two personalities. The first personality despises Isis, but if this personality emerges outside the home it could lead to execution. Therefore a second personality is necessary.*
>
> *That second personality must express an affinity for the militants, and emerges as soon as you see an Isis member or you are stopped at one of their checkpoints. When they ask what you think of Isis, you have to respond in a manner that pleases the militants, so you can pass and get on with your day. You even have to hide your first personality from your children, because militants make a point of asking them if their parents speak ill of the organization …*
>
> *Here, a single mistake can cost a life. But civilians must struggle with internal conflict as well. We have to know when to use which personality, but also ensure that our false personalities don't begin to control our real selves.*[1]

1. Tim Ramadan, "I Am a Civilian in Raqqa. Surviving the Siege Is Becoming Harder Every Day," *Guardian*, August 15, 2017, www.theguardian.com/commentisfree/2017/aug/15/civilian-raqqa-syria-siege-isis-religious-police.

Shown here are the ruins of a home in the city of Raqqa, Syria. ISIS took control of this city in January 2014 and named it the capital of the Islamic State.

claimed that his government would not let Mosul fall "under the shadow of terror and terrorists,"[3] but it seemed impossible to reclaim the city. Capturing Mosul put ISIS on the map, demonstrating to both its followers and its enemies that it was more powerful than many had thought. It was capable of quickly taking command of a geographically important piece of land. Not long after ISIS took Mosul, the group formally announced the establishment of a caliphate in the lands it now controlled and began to refer to itself simply as the Islamic State, although it's still commonly referred to as ISIS as well.

The Caliph Speaks

On July 4, 2014, video of al-Baghdadi was publicly broadcast for the first time. In a sermon at the Great Mosque of al-Nuri in Mosul that he recorded and shared online, he declared himself the ruler of the global caliphate—the leader of Muslims worldwide—and called on his subjects to carry out the holy war against those he considered infidels: "God created us to worship him and spread his religion, and ordered us to fight his enemies for him and for religion."[4]

Al-Baghdadi's sermon was a surprise for those at the mosque. According to a witness, black vehicles with tinted windows pulled up, and men got out chanting, "Allahu Akbar," which means "Allah is great." Those in the mosque were then told that al-Baghdadi would give a sermon and they must listen. Then, civilians in the mosque were kept prisoner for an hour. Gunmen were posted at the doors to block any exit. This sermon symbolized that al-Baghdadi had finally turned Abu Musab al-Zarqawi's vision into a reality. The Islamic State was going global. However, the fear described by some who witnessed the sermon reflected the fact that this was not a reality that was welcomed by all in the Muslim world.

Al-Baghdadi specifically copied the ancient Abbasid caliphs during his sermon. He wore black robes in their honor and even paraphrased what the first caliph—his namesake—said when he succeeded Muhammad: "I was appointed to rule you but I am not the best among you. If you see me acting truly, then follow me. If you see me acting falsely, then advise and guide me … If I disobey God, then do not obey me."[5] Regardless of his words, it was obvious that everyone was expected to obey the new caliph.

After the Islamic State seized Mosul in June 2014, al-Baghdadi and ISIS ruled an area larger than the size of the United Kingdom. This territory was soon filled with fighters from all over the world. Al-Baghdadi's sermon brought thousands of followers to Syria, all of whom were "ready to give up everything at home for a shot at paradise."[6] However, other leaders in the Muslim world stood against the declaration of an Islamic State with al-Baghdadi as caliph.

This screenshot was taken of al-Baghdadi delivering his sermon in Mosul on July 4, 2014. This was the first time the world saw a video of the man who claimed leadership over ISIS.

Al-Baghdadi may have claimed to rule over all Muslims, but in actuality, only a small percentage of the global Muslim community accepted his violent, extremist rule.

Dabiq and the Final Battle

Although Raqqa and Mosul were more strategically important, the capture of the tiny, northern Syrian city Dabiq may have been the most important conquest for the Islamic State from a symbolic standpoint. When Abu Musab al-Zarqawi began the organization that became known as the Islamic State, he said, "The spark has been lit here in Iraq, and its heat will continue to intensify … until it burns the crusader armies in Dabiq."[7] From the very beginning of his terrorist career, al-Zarqawi and his followers preached about the end of the world. Islamic apocalypse prophecies often refer to these "crusader armies" as "Rome," but it is doubtful that they mean the capital city of Italy. Some think references to Rome mean the Eastern Roman Empire, which had its capital in what is now Istanbul, Turkey. Other Muslim sources say that Rome could mean any army of infidels, such as the Americans.

The Islamic State captured Dabiq in August 2014. As an area of great importance leading up to the end of the world, ISIS believed it was necessary to raise the black flag of the caliphate and cleanse the city of sin. In November 2014, ISIS released a video online announcing it had killed a young aid worker and former U.S. Army Ranger named Abdul-Rahman Kassig. The executioner claimed Kassig had been killed in Dabiq, saying, "Here we are, burying the first American Crusader in Dabiq, eagerly waiting for the remainder of your armies to arrive."[8] Many Islamic State followers saw this murder as the beginning of the apocalyptic battle that would bring about the end of the world and eternal victory of Muslims.

The United States Takes Action

The United States had initially been reluctant to use force against ISIS, focusing most of its energy on al-Qaeda and Osama bin Laden until bin Laden's death in 2011. Even after bin Laden was killed by U.S. forces and al-Baghdadi began to grow in power, U.S. leaders

THEY MADE HISTORY: BARACK OBAMA

Born in Hawaii on August 4, 1961, Barack Obama grew up a world away from the White House. However, in 2009, Obama became the first African American to call the White House home as president of the United States.

Obama handled difficult situations at home and abroad while he was president. He helped the country out of a recession and signed the Affordable Care Act to extend health-care coverage to more Americans.

Obama oversaw the military mission that led to the death of Osama bin Laden on May 2, 2011. He also worked to end Syria's use of chemical weapons and led the formation of the global coalition against ISIS. When dealing with Islamist terrorist groups such as al-Qaeda and ISIS, Obama was always quick to remind the American people that the enemy was violent extremism, not Islam. In his address to the nation following bin Laden's death, he stated, "We must also reaffirm

still kept their distance from what was happening in Iraq and Syria. Once the Islamic State took Mosul, though, the previously reluctant U.S. government had to take action.

U.S. president Barack Obama announced that American planes had begun bombing runs in Iraq during the summer of 2014. In response, ISIS murdered its American and European prisoners. In order to mimic the Iraqi prisoners in American custody, the victims were dressed in orange jumpsuits.

In September 2014, a global coalition was announced with the goal of defeating ISIS. Led by the United States, this coalition has worked in both Iraq and Syria to weaken ISIS control in the region. In the United States, the military campaign against ISIS has been named Operation Inherent Resolve and has included steps such as arming Syrian rebels to fight ISIS forces, sending troops into Iraq, and carrying out air strikes against ISIS targets in Iraq and Syria.

that the United States is not—and never will be—at war with Islam."[1]

Obama was the recipient of the Nobel Peace Prize in 2009, and since leaving office in 2017, he and former First Lady Michelle Obama have continued to raise awareness and speak out about important issues in the United States and around the world.

This famous photograph was taken while President Barack Obama, Vice President Joe Biden, Secretary of State Hillary Clinton, and other national security team members watched the raid to catch Osama bin Laden unfold.

1. Quoted in Macon Phillips, "Osama bin Laden Dead," White House, May 2, 2011, obamawhitehouse.archives.gov/blog/2011/05/02/osama-bin-laden-dead.

Although the United States and its allies had finally joined the fight against ISIS, the Islamic State was still in control of large parts of Iraq and Syria as 2014 ended and 2015 began. Life under al-Baghdadi's rule was harsh and difficult, with the threat of violence and death always in the air. However, ISIS used many tactics to keep its power, hold on to its lands, and convince its followers that its path was the right one—even though that path led to brutal violence and horrific human rights abuses.

How You See History

1. Why do you think Abu Muhammad al-Jawlani refused to let Abu Bakr al-Baghdadi join the al-Nusra Front with the Islamic State?
2. Why do you think al-Baghdadi's sermon was so successful at recruiting extremists to his cause?
3. Do you think the United States was too slow to get involved in the fight against ISIS? Why or why not?

CHAPTER FIVE

LIFE UNDER ISIS CONTROL

Abu Bakr al-Baghdadi's sermon on July 4, 2014, was a major turning point in the history of Islamist extremism in the Middle East and around the world. Believers who were already radicalized saw the declaration of an Islamic State as a call to arms. Many of them traveled to Syria and Iraq to join ISIS. Many more Muslims, however, condemned this declaration and al-Baghdadi's violent actions. In addition, foreign governments, including the U.S. government, began to take ISIS much more seriously. The focus of their counterterrorism efforts shifted from al-Qaeda to the Islamic State.

As the Islamic State continued to grow in power, it attracted many to its cause with the promise of apocalyptic glory. Its followers believed they were fighting on the right side of history and would be rewarded when the end of the world came. This fanatical belief in the coming apocalypse meant that al-Baghdadi and his followers didn't care how the world saw them or how many enemies they attracted. In fact, they welcomed battles with foreign forces because they saw them as signs of the end of the world.

Although many ISIS fighters hoped for eternal paradise, the reality of life under ISIS rule in Iraq and Syria in the 2010s was far from it. Harsh punishments, slavery, violence, and destruction became normal parts of life for many during the reign of al-Baghdadi.

Women living under ISIS rule have been forced to follow strict dress codes. They must wear a veil with two layers, a full-body covering, and black gloves. Even showing their eyes can lead to punishment.

Why Do People Join ISIS?

Despite the difficulties of life in the Islamic State, many people traveled from around the world to fight on the side of ISIS. As more enemies considered intervening and attacking the Islamic State, its followers became more convinced and excited that the final battle was approaching—a battle they believed they were destined to win. When the United States began considering military action against the Islamic State in Syria, one ISIS supporter tweeted, "Thirty states remain to complete the number of eighty flags that will gather in Dabiq and begin the battle."[1] This is a reference to an Islamic prophecy that stated Rome would have 80 allies in its battle with the caliphate in Dabiq.

Promising the end of the world has been one of the most powerful ways that ISIS has recruited new extremists. By explicitly claiming that the world is about to end, the group implies that any Muslim who does not help them will be condemned—and any who assists them will be promised a heavenly paradise.

ISIS recruits from many countries have stated that they felt called to gather in Syria and prepare to fight for the cause of an Islamic apocalypse. They abandoned their home countries to fight the final battle against the "infidels" and never expected to return alive, traveling on one-way tickets. One fighter in Syria boasted, "We have here mujahideen from Russia, America, the Philippines, China, Germany, Belgium, Sudan, India and Yemen and other places. They are here because this [is] what the Prophet said and promised, the Grand Battle is happening."[2]

The caliphate promises honor and eternal glory to Islamic youth who may feel isolated from their home societies. A powerful example of the mindset of an ISIS recruit is the story of Abdelaziz Kuwan—a young Muslim from the country of Bahrain who first fought for the al-Nusra Front in Syria. After returning home, he began to feel restless and longed to give up his life for the Islamist cause. He then joined the Islamic State. He was known for his violence and cruelty, which ISIS leaders saw as valuable attributes. He was eventually appointed as a security official. In October 2014, he was shot and killed, but he, like most ISIS fighters, was ready and willing to die for his cause. Jihadists generally write a will, and his was addressed to his mother:

As you know and watch on television channels, the infidels … have gone too far in their oppression, killing, torture, and violations of Muslims' honor. I, by God, cannot see my Muslim sisters and brothers being killed … and I sit without doing anything … I longed for heaven, near the Prophet Muhammad.[3]

Young ISIS fighters like Kuwan feel a serious responsibility to dedicate their time and lives to radical Islam. Although only men are allowed to fight on the front lines for ISIS, women also join the Islamic State. They may not fight, but they serve the men. In addition, one group of women, called the al-Khansa Brigade, polices the behavior of other women. The women in this group are given more power and freedom than other women in the Islamic State.

ISIS recruits believe the end times are near and it is their responsibility to purify the world by killing those they see as infidels—Westerners, Christians, and even other Muslims whose ways and beliefs don't align with those of the Islamic State. They have also openly provoked Western nations with the goal of beginning the final battle. This has created an entirely new kind of public image for a terrorist organization. ISIS does not care about uniting the Muslim world against the West; it cares only about conquering and fighting any group that stands in its way of creating a global caliphate. It also does not care about hiding actions and practices that might earn it more enemies, especially in the Muslim world.

Even though the Islamic State has demonstrated that it does not care about its public reputation, it has attempted to show that it cares about those who pledge allegiance to its organization. For example, it recorded videos of food being handed out to those in need and general examples of what might be seen as humanitarian

Although ISIS fighters welcome war and destruction as a sign of the end of the world, civilians living under the flag of the Islamic State have suffered greatly from the violence around them.

relief. These small efforts, however, are more like propaganda than the truth—the quality of life for people in Iraq and Syria greatly diminished under ISIS control.

Ruling by Fear

Where the Islamic State moved in, communities suffered. Those groups who cooperated and handed over their territory willingly were given some money and basic necessities. The Islamic State collected taxes and provided some services for those under its control who followed its strict interpretation of sharia law.

Anyone who did not cooperate, though, was punished, and in some cases that meant death, kidnapping, or enslavement. The Islamic State has enforced *hudud* punishments, which are specific penalties described directly in the Quran or interpreted from other Islamic sources. These include death for speaking against Islam, homosexual acts, treason, and murder; death by stoning for those who have committed adultery; and amputation of a hand for stealing. In addition, crucifixion—the killing of a person by nailing or tying them to a cross—is a common way the death penalty is carried out by ISIS, especially for those who are put to death for being Christians. The Islamic State has carried out these death sentences publicly and forced crowds of civilians to watch to terrify everyone into submission. In some cases, ISIS has broadcast its killings on social media to send a message to those who stand against the Islamic State.

Al-Baghdadi's strict interpretation of sharia law has even been applied to dress codes for areas under ISIS control. According to ISIS, men can't wear Western clothing, and women must be completely covered by long dresses, veils, and gloves. In addition, ISIS states that women should not be allowed in public without a male chaperone. Smoking cigarettes is punishable in the eyes of ISIS by whipping, severing fingers, or jail time.

Slavery in the Islamic State

The treatment of women in the Islamic State has been a cause of global concern for many years, and one of the most disturbing violations of women by ISIS is its adoption of the practice of slavery. In 2014, the Islamic State publicly reinstated the acceptance of slavery,

FROM THE SOURCE: WOMEN PUNISHING WOMEN

In 2019, the news source Al Jazeera compiled stories from women who'd lived under ISIS control. The following story comes from a woman named Aisha, who lived in Raqqa and was trained by ISIS to police the women around her and to punish those who broke the rules of sharia law. She described some of the crimes women were found guilty of under her watch:

> *If a woman walked down the street unaccompanied, she was arrested. She had to be accompanied by her brother or husband. If a woman walked alone or took a taxi without them, she was arrested.*
>
> *We were supposed to patrol the neighbourhoods, the markets, to look for women whose clothes did not conform to [ISIS's] laws …*
>
> *Once they arrived at the station, the women were flogged [whipped]. They were kept in prison for a few days. Then they made the women buy regulation clothing from them before releasing them.*
>
> *One day, we arrested a woman who was wearing nail polish. They used a pair of pliers to pull out her nails …*
>
> *The women who were members of [ISIS] banned everyone from smoking, but they themselves smoked. In fact, I would buy their cigarettes for them. They banned alcohol but they drank. It was fine for them, but a sin for everyone else.*[1]

1. Quoted in "Women Under ISIL: The Torturers," Al Jazeera, November 27, 2019, www.aljazeera.com/indepth/features/women-isil-torturers-191124095032690.html.

especially of women. Although slavery is considered illegal in other Muslim nations, ISIS leaders stated that their interpretation of sharia law allowed for the enslavement of people. A spokesperson for ISIS promised, "We will conquer your Rome, break your crosses, and enslave your women. If we do not reach that time, then our children

Human rights group are working hard to rescue and help members of the Yazidi community, such as the women and children shown here, who were captured and enslaved by ISIS.

and grandchildren will reach it, and they will sell your sons as slaves at the slave market."[4]

In 2016, a UN report estimated that ISIS enslaved 3,500 people Most of these enslaved people were women and children from the Yazidi community. Yazidism is an ancient religion whose followers live primarily in Iraq. The religion takes pieces from Christianity, Islam, and Judaism, as well as elements of ancient Iranian religions such as Zoroastrianism. Believers are unjustly considered devil-worshippers by some and have suffered persecution for centuries. They are largely Kurds, a people most closely related to Iranians, and they are a minority in Iraq. Al-Qaeda and ISIS declared Yazidis infidels. They have been killed in large numbers by Islamist terrorist groups, and they have also been the victims of brutal human rights abuses, including being sold into slavery.

Young Yazidi boys were often kidnapped and trained to be child soldiers for ISIS. They were tortured and brainwashed into believing ISIS was right and their Yazidi family and friends were infidels. As Kimberly Dozier reported for *TIME* magazine:

> *The terrorists separated [Yazidi] children from their families, sometimes killing their parents in front of them. In the soil of that trauma, they planted the idea that the boys were the future army of ISIS, indoctrinating them with the arrogance of conquerors. They laced the boys' food with Captagon, an amphetamine [a stimulant drug], to dull their fear and trained some as suicide attackers. Many more were sent to the front lines where fighting was bloodiest, forced to wear suicide belts at all times, with instructions to blow themselves up if the enemy got too close.*[5]

Young Yazidi girls suffered in a different way. Along with adult Yazidi women, they were enslaved and offered as "gifts" to ISIS fighters. They often endured violence and abuse at the hands of their captors, who saw them as their property and not as human beings.

A Campaign of Cultural Destruction

ISIS has taken much from the people of Iraq and Syria—their lands, their freedom, and sometimes even their lives. It has also taken reminders of their history and culture. The Middle East is rich in ancient archaeological sites that contain old and valuable pieces of art and architecture. ISIS has allowed people to dig in the ancient sites that it controls, as long as the Islamic State is given a certain percentage of the value of whatever is found. ISIS even encouraged field crews to dig in some parts of the area surrounding the Euphrates River in hopes that a valuable discovery would be made that could be sold on the black market to help fund its terrorist activities.

Not all of the Islamic State's cultural destruction is for profit, however. In March 2015, ISIS posted a video online showing a group of soldiers destroying the archaeological site of the Iraqi city of Nimrud. This city had an archaeological history dating back 3,000 years, and before its destruction, the government of Iraq had nominated it to be included on the United Nations Educational, Scientific and Cultural Organization's (UNESCO's) list of World Heritage sites. Regardless, ISIS used sledgehammers, power tools, and explosives to destroy the cultural artifacts found there. The UN stated that the major, deliberate cultural destruction was a war crime.

In another online video, ISIS supporters demolished artifacts at a museum in Mosul. In the video, an ISIS fighter explained the reasoning behind the destruction of cultural and historical sites: "These antiquities and idols behind me were from people in past centuries and were worshiped instead of God. When God Almighty orders us to destroy these statues, idols and antiquities, we must do it, even if they're worth billions of dollars."[6] ISIS has also burned thousands of books and rare texts in the Mosul Library, in what UNESCO said is "one of the most devastating acts of destruction of library collections in human history."[7]

The Islamic State considers all religious shrines to be idolatrous—promoting the worship of something other than Allah. It has destroyed many religious buildings—not just Christian

Shown here is the aftermath of ISIS's destruction of Nimrud. This ancient city was known for paintings called frescoes, but these were destroyed under the eye of the Islamic State.

churches and Jewish temples, but also Muslim mosques. The Islamic State has been focused on eliminating any evidence that there is another way to practice Islam—through peace and appreciation of culture—as opposed to violence and destruction.

After ISIS lost its hold on these lands, UNESCO and other groups began the long, painful, and expensive process of trying to reconstruct these pieces of history. Although some progress has already been made, the road to rebuilding will be long, and some artifacts and pieces of cultural heritage will never be recovered.

Welcoming Conflict

Every person murdered or enslaved and every important piece of ancient history destroyed or sold creates an enemy against ISIS. The Islamic State has made enemies of the Kurds, Yazidis, Christians, Muslims, and even its former parent group, al-Qaeda. It has united almost every nearby ethnic and religious group against it. Countries across the world, such as the United States and the entire continent of Europe, oppose the Islamic State, and some have fought back against ISIS through military action.

When ISIS beheaded the American journalist James Foley in 2014, the United States led a series of air strikes that killed thousands of Islamic State fighters. When ISIS burned Jordanian pilot Muath al-Kaseasbeh alive in 2015, Jordan increased its efforts in the fight against the Islamic State. When ISIS beheaded 21 Egyptians in Libya that same year, Egypt responded by dropping bombs on ISIS camps in Libya. Most of the world is unified in standing against this terrorist organization.

Leaders and supporters of ISIS have never seemed intimidated by the global coalition against them. In fact, they welcome the

HISTORY HAPPENED HERE: PALMYRA

One of the main cultural sites ISIS attacked in Syria was the ancient archaeological site of Palmyra. It stood for thousands of years as a major settlement due to its water sources and fertile soil. It was also an important location on trade routes linking various groups, including the Romans, Persians, Indians, and Chinese. Its location at this cultural crossroads allowed it to flourish as a center of art and architecture, featuring monuments, temples, and sculptures. The buildings and artwork found in Palmyra became known for their blending of Roman and Persian influences.

Palmyra was named to the UNESCO World Heritage List in 1980 for its outstanding universal value as a cultural landmark. However, when ISIS took over the area around Palmyra, it destroyed much of the site. After years of fighting around Palmyra, the Syrian government officially reclaimed the site in March 2017. UNESCO then began working on a plan to restore Palmyra, and restoration efforts are continuing as of 2021.

The Temple of Bel was once a prominent part of Palmyra, but this is all that was left of it after ISIS destroyed the site.

conflict as a sign of the apocalypse and proudly boast about their attacks and numerous human rights abuses. They use social media to share videos of beheadings, messages supporting slavery, and calls for violence against all they see as infidels.

The Islamic State's public displays of brutality have earned it many enemies, but also many recruits. Social media and other parts

PAST MEETS PRESENT: REVIVE THE SPIRIT OF MOSUL

When ISIS destroyed many of Mosul's museums, libraries, mosques, and other cultural centers, the second largest Iraqi city suffered losses that many weren't sure it could come back from. The symbolic attacks on the city's heritage created a sense of lost identity, but after the Iraqi government retook Mosul in 2017, groups immediately began working to restore what had been lost.

The biggest project to help Mosul recover from the devastation it suffered under ISIS is being led by UNESCO. It's called Revive the Spirit of Mosul, and according to the UNESCO website, "Reviving Mosul is not only about reconstructing heritage sites, it is about empowering the population as agents of change involved in the process of rebuilding their city through culture and education."[1]

There are three main parts to the Revive the Spirit of Mosul project. The first is the rebuilding and restoration of the city's heritage sites that were damaged, including the Great Mosque of al-Nuri. The second involves creating a strong education system, and the third calls for the reopening of museums, libraries, and other cultural sites.

1. Quoted in "Revive the Spirit of Mosul," UNESCO, en.unesco.org/fieldoffice/baghdad/revivemosul (accessed May 21, 2020).

of the digital world have allowed ISIS to spread its message to people in countries far from Iraq and Syria. Some of these people have traveled to the Middle East to fight for the caliphate, but others have carried out attacks inspired by ISIS in their home countries. Attacks by ISIS supporters on the Western world, including the United States, have created a global conflict and led to a new era in the international fight against terrorism.

THEY MADE HISTORY: JAMES FOLEY

The death of James Foley was a turning point in the American public's understanding of ISIS. Foley, who was born on October 18, 1973, worked to educate young people, mothers, and people in prison before beginning his career as a journalist.

Foley was a conflict journalist who reported from places such as Afghanistan and Libya, where he was held by the government for 44 days before being released. Finally, he traveled to Syria to report on the civil war in that country. On November 22, 2012, Foley disappeared. He was held captive by ISIS for two years. The group asked for money in exchange for his release, but the U.S. government didn't negotiate with ISIS.

On August 19, 2014, ISIS shared a video in which Foley was beheaded on camera. His tragic death alerted many Americans to the brutality of ISIS. Following his murder, his family started the James W. Foley Legacy Foundation. The goal of the foundation is to advocate for people still being held hostage and to educate journalists about how to stay as safe as possible in danger zones such as Syria.

How You See History

1. Why do you think so many foreigners were inspired to travel to Iraq and Syria to fight for ISIS?
2. What do you think is the biggest reason behind ISIS's destruction of cultural and historic sites?
3. Why does ISIS post so much of its brutality online, when other terrorist organizations and violent governments throughout history often tried to hide their war crimes and human rights abuses?

TOUS ENSEMBLE
22.03.2016
St. Martin
CLUB
Sailing Crew
PROJECT BOAT N°129

CHAPTER SIX

A GLOBAL THREAT

As ISIS grew in power in Iraq and Syria, it also grew in influence around the world. It has been the driving force behind some of the deadliest and most infamous terrorist attacks in the 21st century. Some have been carried out by terrorists directly connected with ISIS; others have been carried out by "lone wolves" who've been inspired by the hateful, violent messages ISIS shares online. The internet has made it possible for many people to be radicalized by ISIS propaganda without ever setting foot in Iraq or Syria. These radicals then act in the name of ISIS, pledging their loyalty to the organization before—or sometimes even during—their attacks.

ISIS has proudly and publicly claimed responsibility for bombings, shootings, and other brutal acts of violence around the world. It has turned airports, government buildings, concerts, and places of worship into battlegrounds in its fight against those it sees as infidels. ISIS attacks in France, Belgium, Egypt, and numerous other countries have claimed many lives and spread fear through many cities and communities, and world leaders are working hard to find new ways to combat these new threats.

Memorials have been set up around the world to honor those who've lost their lives in attacks carried out and inspired by ISIS. Shown here is a memorial to the victims of bombings in Brussels, Belgium, that were carried out by ISIS followers in 2016.

North American Attacks

One of the first known attacks inspired by ISIS on a Western target took place in Canada in 2014. On October 22, Michael Zehaf-Bibeau shot and killed Nathan Cirillo, a Canadian soldier, at the National War Memorial in Ottawa, Ontario. After that, he attacked Parliament Hill, which is the seat of the Canadian federal government. He was killed by security forces before he could take any more lives, but his actions were praised by ISIS.

Americans have also been the victims of attacks inspired by ISIS. On December 2, 2015, Tashfeen Malik and Syed Rizwan Farook—a married couple—opened fire at an office holiday party in San Bernardino, California. They killed 14 people and injured 21 others before being killed by police. According to some sources, a post on Facebook was made during the attack in which Malik—or possibly both shooters—pledged allegiance to ISIS. Following the attack, ISIS did not directly claim responsibility but instead called the killers supporters of the Islamic State. The San Bernardino massacre showed the American public that ISIS didn't have to directly order an attack to be behind an act of terror. By supporting lone wolf attacks—attacks carried out by individuals or small groups without a larger connection to ISIS—the organization has inspired many to commit terrible acts of violence in its name.

Another terrorist who referenced ISIS during his killing of innocent victims was Omar Mateen. On June 12, 2016, Mateen killed 49 people at an Orlando, Florida, nightclub called Pulse, which was frequented by members of the LGBTQ+ community. Mateen held people hostage in the club for hours, and during this time, he called 911 to pledge allegiance to Abu Bakr al-Baghdadi. According to some sources, he also told hostage negotiators that he was acting in response to U.S. military actions in Iraq and Syria. At

The Pulse nightclub shooting was an attack on members of the LGBTQ+ community. After the shooting, people across the United States and around the world gathered to show their support for this community.

PAST MEETS PRESENT: ISIS AND ISLAMOPHOBIA

ISIS attacks on the Western world have contributed to a rise in the hatred and fear of Muslims known as Islamophobia. Although most Muslims around the world stand against ISIS, some people have ignorantly grouped all Muslims together and believe ISIS represents the views of the global Muslim community. This has led to instances of Muslim women having their head coverings ripped off, immigrants from Muslim-majority countries being discriminated against, and people who look like they might be from the Middle East—even if they were born in the United States—being told to go back to their country.

In some cases, Islamophobia has led to violence. In the United States, hate crimes against Muslims have risen dramatically in recent years. This isn't just an American problem, though. In European countries, Islamophobia is also strong, and it's especially visible in demonstrations against refugees from Syria. In addition, in New Zealand, a March 2019 attack on two mosques left 51 people dead in an act of Islamophobic violence.

ISIS welcomes Islamophobia. According to Yousef bin Ahmed al-Othaimeen, the secretary general for the Organisation of Islamic Cooperation:

> *ISIS's chief strategists set out to destroy "the grey zone," the peaceful co-existence between Muslims and non-Muslims in Western societies. But they could not do so alone. They needed Western societies to become unwitting partners in their plans. They sought to provoke Islamophobia through brutal acts of terrorism, which would turn Westerners against their innocent, often upstanding Muslim neighbors.*[1]

By working to demolish dangerous stereotypes and fighting against violence and hatred fueled by both Islamist extremism and Islamophobia, people around the world can help ensure global cooperation in the fight against ISIS.

1. Yousef bin Ahmed Al-Othaimeen, "Anti-Muslim Policies Help ISIS with Its Goal," *TIME*, March 28, 2017, time.com/4699591/isis-far-right-islamophobia/.

the time, this shooting was the most deadly mass shooting in U.S. history and the most deadly terrorist attack on U.S. soil since the 9/11 attacks.

France Becomes a Battleground

Tensions between Muslims and non-Muslims in France existed long before ISIS. In 2004, the nation banned Muslim head coverings in public schools as part of a ban on all overt religious symbols, including Christian crosses. It has since banned coverings, such as the burqa, in all public places, which sparked protests from Muslims and others who believe this violates religious freedom.

In January 2015, 12 people were killed at the offices of the French magazine *Charlie Hebdo*, which has been known to make fun of religious figures, including the Prophet Muhammad. Although an offshoot of al-Qaeda took responsibility for this attack, a friend of the two men who carried out the *Charlie Hebdo* shooting later killed four hostages in a kosher grocery store in Paris. This attack was believed to have been inspired by ISIS and not by al-Qaeda.

Months later, Paris would be the sight of even more tragedy. On November 13, 2015, a series of coordinated attacks in Paris killed 130 people and wounded hundreds more. The attackers carried out shootings and suicide bombings that targeted people at restaurants and bars, as well as those watching a soccer game between France and Germany. The greatest loss of life was experienced inside the Bataclan concert hall, where the American band Eagles of Death Metal was performing. Concertgoers were held hostage in the building until French police stormed the hall. It was later reported that 90 people were killed in the Bataclan. ISIS claimed responsibility for this carefully planned and executed attack.

Another deadly attack took place in the French city of Nice on July 14, 2016. That day is known as Bastille Day—a national holiday in France—and a large crowd had gathered to watch fireworks. Mohamed Lahouaiej-Bouhlel drove a truck into this crowd and killed 84 people. Hundreds more were injured. After the attack, a news network that supports ISIS shared the following message: "The person who carried out the operation in Nice, France, to run down

Barack Obama was president of the United States at the time of the 2015 attacks on Paris. He visited a memorial to the victims when he traveled to the city weeks later to pay his respects to those who lost their lives.

people was one of the soldiers of Islamic State. He carried out the operation in response to calls to target nationals of states that are part of the coalition fighting Islamic State."[1]

Truck attacks such as the one in Nice were carried out in other places, too, including New York City and London, England. ISIS has encouraged its supporters to use this method of attack because it is relatively easy to carry out and can cause a lot of damage. However, methods such as barriers and greater security screenings for vehicles approaching mass gatherings have now been put in place in an attempt to stop these kinds of attacks.

Terror Throughout Europe

ISIS also claimed responsibility for a truck attack that killed 12 people at a Christmas market in Berlin, Germany, in December 2016. The following year, Christmas markets throughout Europe, which are popular gathering places during the holiday season, were placed on high alert following direct threats from ISIS.

Airports were also a cause for concern as potential targets in Europe, following the 2016 ISIS bombing of an airport in Brussels, Belgium. The two bombs that were set off there, as well as a third that was set off at a subway station, left 32 people dead and more than 300 people wounded. At the time, it was the deadliest terrorist attack in Belgium's history.

One of the most infamous ISIS attacks in Europe took place in Manchester, England, in May 2017. As people were leaving a concert by American singer Ariana Grande, a man identified by ISIS as "one of the soldiers of the caliphate"[2] detonated a bomb that killed 22 people and injured more than 50 people. Many of those who witnessed the horrible aftermath of the attack were young fans of Grande's. Grande herself has stated that she has dealt with

HISTORY HAPPENED HERE: THE BATACLAN

The Bataclan had a rich cultural history before the 2015 ISIS attacks, and Parisians hope that it will be known once again for its role as a cultural site and not the site of a tragedy.

The Bataclan was designed in 1864 by Charles Duval, and it was built in a Chinese style. It was originally a music hall with a café and space for dancing, but it was later converted into a movie theater. By the 1970s, the Bataclan had been transformed once again into a concert venue that hosted rock and roll acts such as the Ramones and Prince.

Following the terrorist attacks of November 13, 2015, the Bataclan closed for a year. It reopened with a concert featuring the famous musical artist Sting. Today, it's still known as a concert venue and also features a memorial plaque honoring those who lost their lives there in 2015.

post-traumatic stress disorder because of the events of that night. She has worked to raise money for those injured in the bombing and for the families of the victims.

Throughout the 2010s, other attacks inspired by ISIS continued to terrorize parts of Europe. Stabbings, shootings, and truck attacks led to tighter security measures in public places, counterterrorism raids, and stronger cooperation between other countries as they worked to push back against the influence of ISIS in Europe.

Attacks in Asia and Africa

Parts of Asia and Africa were also affected by ISIS attacks throughout the 2010s. The targets included places as different as a Starbucks in Jakarta, Indonesia, and the parliament building in Iran. In the attack in Jakarta, which took place in 2016, ISIS supporters attacked an area around a Starbucks and department store, killing two people before killing themselves in a suicide bombing. In Iran, guns and suicide bombings were responsible for the deaths of 12 people in a 2017 attack on the legislative headquarters of the country and the

FROM THE SOURCE: JOE BIDEN ON THE PARIS ATTACKS

After the ISIS attacks on Paris in November 2015, Joe Biden, who was vice president of the United States at the time, offered the following words of support to the American and French people:

> *I join President Obama in offering my deepest condolences to all those wounded and to the families who lost loved ones in today's terrorist attacks in Paris. It's heartbreaking. Outrageous. The American people understand and share the pain the people of Paris are going through … And, as we've done before, in the face of dangers and threats, we will look out for one another. We will stand together. We will never bow. We will never break. That's the character of our two nations. We are bound by timeless democratic values that … extremist networks can never match, wherever they are … We will respond. We will overcome. We will endure.*[1]

1. Quoted in Melanie Garunay, "President Obama Offers a Statement on the Attacks in Paris. Watch Here," The White House, November 13, 2015, obamawhitehouse.archives.gov/blog/2015/11/13/watch-president-obamas-statement-attacks-paris.

tomb of Ayatollah Khomeini, who was the founder of the Islamic Republic of Iran and a Shia Muslim.

Places of worship have been frequent targets of ISIS in Asia and Africa. For example, in 2018, Indonesia was once again targeted by ISIS. In attacks on three Christian churches in the country, more than 10 people were killed. These bombings were carried out by families, including young children.

The following year, churches were again targeted—this time in Sri Lanka. In coordinated attacks on Easter Sunday church services, hotels, and a housing complex, more than 350 people were killed. ISIS took credit for the suicide bombings, claiming those who carried out the attacks were fighting for the Islamic State.

The Eiffel Tower in Paris shut off its lights after ISIS killed more than 300 people in an Egyptian mosque in 2017. This was done to show that the people of Paris were mourning along with the people of Egypt.

ISIS destroyed mosques in Iraq and Syria, and it also did this in other countries. One of the most tragic examples of an ISIS attack on a mosque took place in Egypt in November 2017. More than 300 people were killed in an attack on a mosque that was frequented by those who practiced the Sufi branch of Islam. The Sufi branch—like the Shia sect of Islam—has been targeted by ISIS because the Islamic State believes their way of practicing Islam is the only correct way.

New Battlefields

Governments, counterterrorism units, and militaries around the world have improved their ability to find suspected ISIS supporters and stop terror attacks before they're carried out, but ISIS supporters have still been carrying out acts of violence against foreign targets. In January 2020, ISIS claimed responsibility for an attack on a mosque in Pakistan that killed at least 15 people. The attack is believed to have been directed at members of the Taliban who frequent the mosque. ISIS and the Taliban are fighting to control parts of Afghanistan.

Afghanistan has become a new battlefield for the Islamic State in recent years, as supporters of ISIS and its affiliates, or related groups, carry out suicide attacks on targets such as Shia communities in the country. In addition, the North African nation of Libya has also seen increased attention from the Islamic State. Like Iraq and Syria, Libya is a nation struggling with instability, which has made it a place where Islamist extremism can flourish.

It may seem as if ISIS has the ability to inspire many people to commit acts of terrorism. However, it's important to remember that the vast majority of Muslims around the world are peaceful people. ISIS has far more people fighting against it than for it, and because of this, its power and influence have been declining in recent years. As ISIS lost land in Iraq and Syria, the future of the caliphate began to seem uncertain.

How You See History

1. Why do you think ISIS wants Islamophobia to spread around the world?
2. What steps can people take to support communities and individuals who've been affected by acts of terrorism?
3. Do you remember hearing or reading about any of the attacks mentioned in this chapter while you were growing up? If you do, how did you feel at the time?

CHAPTER SEVEN

THE FUTURE OF ISIS

ISIS reached the height of its power in Iraq and Syria in 2015. By the end of that year, it had begun losing its hold on its lands, struggling to fight back against Iraqi, Syrian, and coalition forces on multiple fronts. The Islamic State continued to shrink in the following years, and by 2018, President Donald Trump had declared that ISIS had been defeated.

Trump's optimism wasn't shared by everyone, though. It soon became clear that, while ISIS had lost its lands in Iraq and Syria, it hadn't been completely eliminated. Pockets of strong ISIS support still exist in the Middle East, and foreign followers are still being radicalized around the world on social media. Even the death of al-Baghdadi didn't destroy ISIS; it named a new leader and vowed to continue its mission.

The battle against ISIS isn't over. However, for many of the Iraqi and Syrian citizens who've been freed from the rule of the Islamic State, the long process of rebuilding their cities and their lives has begun.

Losing Ground in Iraq

Iraq was where ISIS had first developed, but by 2016, it was also where it began to see significant losses in its territory. By early 2016, ISIS had been driven out of the city of Ramadi, and by the summer of that year, Fallujah was once again in the hands of the Iraqi government.

U.S. air strikes aided Iraqi fighters against ISIS, helping to reclaim Iraqi cities and taking out ISIS leaders. The United States backed a

◀ In 2017, the Islamic State abandoned its capital of Raqqa. However, people living in Raqqa are still surrounded by reminders of the violence that city experienced as the former capital of the Islamic State.

PAST MEETS PRESENT: DOMESTIC TERRORISM IN THE UNITED STATES

Despite the decline in ISIS's power and influence in recent years, many Americans still think of foreign Islamist extremists as the most likely group to carry out terrorist attacks in the United States. However, recent evidence shows this belief is incorrect. According to a report in *TIME* magazine, far-right extremists have carried out almost three times as many terrorist attacks in the United States as Islamist extremists since 9/11. Far-right extremists typically hold very conservative political views, including a strong belief in white nationalism and anti-immigrant policies.

According to the Federal Bureau of Investigation (FBI), domestic terrorism is on the rise in the United States. Domestic terrorism has many different definitions, but generally it involves a citizen carrying out an act of terrorism in their own country. While the threat of foreign Islamist extremists carrying out a terrorist attack in the United States should still be taken seriously, domestic terrorism has become an even greater threat to Americans.

Law enforcement agencies around the country are working to develop stronger policies to stop domestic terrorism in its tracks. Experts have stated that the fight against domestic terrorism begins with a stronger understanding of exactly what it is. Calling these acts of violence by the correct name, instead of calling attacks only by Islamist extremists "terrorism," is the first step toward fighting this growing problem.

major Iraqi offensive in late 2016 to take back the most important city held by ISIS in Iraq: Mosul. The battle for that city raged on for nine months, and some experts have reported that between 5,000 and 11,000 civilians lost their lives in the brutal fighting. PBS correspondent Jane Ferguson reported:

> *The battle for Mosul was one of the most brutal urban warfare campaigns in modern history. U.S.-led coalition warplanes dropped*

Years after ISIS forces were driven out of Mosul, the destruction caused by the battle for the city can still be seen.

bombs that leveled building after building. Iraqi troops are believed to have endured casualty rates not seen since World War II.

The government banned filming of injured soldiers and never released the real numbers of its troops killed in battle. But it was civilians, trapped inside this killing field, who paid the highest price, in part due to an easing of the rules of engagement for U.S. military strikes, as the fight for Mosul began.[1]

On July 9, 2017, the Iraqi prime minister Haider al-Abadi declared an Iraqi victory in the battle for Mosul. However, fighting still continued throughout Iraq. ISIS fighters were prepared to die for their cause, and suicide attacks were still common Islamic State battle tactics. Despite its desperate fighting—and the loss of Iraqi lives left in its wake—the Islamic State continued to lose its grip on Iraq throughout 2017.

In November 2017, Iraqi forces took back the town of Rawa, which was the last town controlled by ISIS in Iraq. Then, in December, al-Abadi officially declared that all of Iraq had been liberated from ISIS control. However, ISIS supporters still exist in the country and have continued to fight back using guerrilla warfare and terrorist attacks. Creating a sense of stability in Iraq has been deemed essential to prevent ISIS from regaining power in the region, making Iraq a continued place of importance in the global fight against ISIS.

Struggles in Syria

While ISIS was losing ground in Iraq, it was also facing struggles in Syria. In 2016, ISIS was forced out of Dabiq. This was a significant symbolic defeat because Dabiq was such an important part of the apocalyptic prophecies ISIS used to legitimize its rule.

Dabiq was one of many areas in Syria that ISIS was forced to give up in the following years. The Syrian Democratic Forces (SDF) were the group most directly responsible for fighting ISIS on the ground in Syria. These rebels, who are mainly Kurdish and Arab, have been backed by the United States and led the push to free many Syrian cities from ISIS control. This includes the former ISIS

THEY MADE HISTORY: NADIA MURAD

Even after ISIS was driven out of Iraq's major cities, the trauma the group caused remained. Nadia Murad is one of many people working to help civilians who were harmed during ISIS's campaign of terror in Iraq.

Murad was born in Iraq in 1993 and belonged to the Yazidi community. In 2014, ISIS took control of the part of Iraq she called home. She was kidnapped and forced into slavery, enduring abuse for three months before she escaped.

Following her escape from her ISIS captors, Murad began speaking out about slavery and the crimes ISIS committed against the Yazidi people. She has worked closely with the United Nations to support victims of human trafficking—the illegal transporting of people, often for forced labor. She is also the head of Nadia's Initiative, which is an organization dedicated to working with governments to help the Yazidi people and survivors of the kind of abuse she endured under ISIS.

In 2017, she shared her story with the world in the book *The Last Girl: My Story of Captivity, and My Fight Against the Islamic State*. The next year, she was awarded the Nobel Peace Prize for her work on behalf of the Yazidi community and all victims of human trafficking and slavery, especially women.

Nadia Murad is working to create a world where no more women have to suffer what she went through when ISIS invaded her hometown.

capital of Raqqa. In late 2016, the SDF started a campaign to reclaim Raqqa. By isolating the city, the SDF weakened ISIS's control over the region around Raqqa. In addition, the U.S.-led coalition carried out air strikes in and around the ISIS capital, but they had a negative consequence. According to some human rights monitoring groups, these air strikes killed more than 1,000 civilians.

In October 2017, the SDF declared victory in Raqqa. ISIS had been driven from its own capital. Later in 2017, the Syrian government stated that ISIS had been defeated throughout the country. However, like in Iraq, small areas of ISIS support remain in Syria, and fighters continue to carry out smaller attacks.

ISIS officially lost all its territory in Iraq and Syria following the fall of the Syrian village of Baghouz to the SDF in March 2019. The Islamic State could no longer claim to be a physical caliphate; all its lands had been reclaimed by Iraq and Syria. This didn't mean, though, that it was dead. Not even the death of its leader could bring ISIS down for good.

The Fall of the Caliph

ISIS dealt with another major blow in October 2019, when Abu Bakr al-Baghdadi was killed following a raid by U.S. forces. As the forces closed in, al-Baghdadi reportedly detonated a suicide vest, killing himself before the troops could get to him. Al-Baghdadi's death was seen as an important victory in the continuing fight against ISIS, and it was followed by reports of the death of his likely successor, Abu Hassan al-Muhajir. He had been an official spokesperson for ISIS, and he was killed in a separate raid soon after al-Baghdadi's death.

Although ISIS seemed to have lost its two most important leaders, it didn't take long to appoint a new caliph. Abu Ibrahim al-Hashimi al-Qurashi was named caliph days after the deaths of al-Baghdadi and al-Muhajir. Not much was revealed about his identity—even to followers of the Islamic State. It's believed, though, that his real name is Amir Muhammad Sa'id Abdal-Rahman al-Mawla (with many alternate spellings presented by various news outlets). According to the British newspaper *The Guardian*, he was behind the campaign to eliminate and enslave the Yazidi people.

In an official audio recording, a spokesperson for ISIS warned the United States not to celebrate the death of al-Baghdadi. The basic ruling structure of ISIS seemed to still be in place, and experts believed that meant it was still a threat that should be taken seriously.

Still a Threat

Although Donald Trump stated that ISIS had been defeated during his presidency, his opinion was not shared by counterterrorism experts. In January 2020, the UN released a report about the status of ISIS in Iraq and Syria. It found that ISIS fighters were growing increasingly bold in their attacks in these nations under their new leadership. The UN warned that ISIS was planning to exploit continued instability in Iraq and Syria to regain its strength.

Conditions in the camps where relatives of ISIS fighters are held are often poor.

In places such as Raqqa, which saw heavy bombing from coalition forces, some citizens miss the stability the Islamic State provided and blame the poverty and destruction around them on the Americans. As one resident of Raqqa explained:

> *ISIS is terrorism, there's no doubt about that. Despite this, life was better then. It's very expensive now. Bread under ISIS was cheaper. Now some families can't even afford that ... If the U.S. and the local government here don't fix things, then in the end the people will rebel. The pressures will cause people to explode.*[2]

The UN also warned that ISIS has been calling for its fighters who've been held in prisons to be broken out. Prison camps allowed early Islamic State leaders to gain followers and radicalize other Muslims, and experts believe this problem has the potential to continue in today's detention centers. In camps where the families of ISIS fighters are being held, there's a high potential for people—especially young men—to be radicalized and inspired to carry on the mission of ISIS.

Capitalizing on Chaos

As 2020 continued, ISIS seemed to be regaining some of its strength. The group began carrying out IED attacks and other, more sophisticated operations in Iraq and Syria once again. In addition, the COVID-19 pandemic that infected millions around the world in 2020 had another dangerous side

As COVID-19 swept through Syria, some displaced persons returned to their cities, which had been damaged by ISIS and U.S. air strikes, rather than staying in crowded camps, where they were more likely to get sick.

FROM THE SOURCE: INSIDE THE AL-HOL CAMP

One of the camps housing the families of ISIS fighters in Syria is known as al-Hol. There's a stark divide in the camp between women who still practice the radical, extremist Islamist beliefs of ISIS and those who do not, and NPR reporter Jane Arraf described this divide:

> *This is the foreigners section of al-Hol camp. It's home to 11,000 women and children from more than 30 countries—women who came joyfully, believing they were fulfilling the will of God; women forced or tricked by their husbands into coming. And in a part of the camp known as Australia Street, outside a tent where the roof is sagging from the rain, there's a group of women who want me to know they don't belong here …*
>
> *Inside, the women are dressed in regular clothes, the Australian woman in a low-cut purple top. But outside, they all wear long cloaks and cover their faces. They say if they don't, there are women in the camp who will label them infidels. Some women have been killed. One was cut into pieces …*
>
> *All of the women who will talk to us say they never fought for ISIS. It's impossible to tell and difficult to imagine what will happen to this generation of young children born in the ISIS caliphate.*[1]

1. Jane Arraf, "Conditions Deteriorate at Syrian Camp Where ISIS Families Are Held," NPR, December 23, 2019, www.npr.org/2019/12/23/790687279/conditions-deteriorate-at-syrian-camp-where-isis-families-are-held.

effect: emboldening ISIS. As forces in Iraq and Syria had to turn their attention to the pandemic, ISIS fighters were able to carry out more attacks and regroup in some areas they had once controlled.

In addition, the protests against racial inequality and police brutality that swept across the United States starting in May 2020 created the kind of chaos ISIS often uses to its advantage. Reports from counterterrorism officials in New York City stated that terrorist organizations such as ISIS were using the protests to recruit more followers and call for lone-wolf attacks at these demonstrations.

The attack on the U.S. Capitol on January 6, 2021, by insurrectionists proved that the United States is still vulnerable to acts of terror—both foreign and domestic. Some national security experts have worried that this display of domestic terrorism could inspire ISIS followers and provide a kind of example for them to follow in the future.

What Does the Future Hold?

The future of the fight against ISIS depends on a strong understanding of its past. When examining the creation of ISIS and other terrorist organizations, it's clear that unstable conditions in certain countries allowed these organizations to grow and gain followers. This is why experts warn that promoting stability in Iraq and Syria today is so important. If these countries continue to struggle to recover from years of war, it will be easier for ISIS to regain the power it lost.

ISIS is unique in its methods, its recruitment, and the things it is fighting for. Learning as much as possible about ISIS fighters has allowed military experts and counterterrorism officials to become better at stopping these fighters from carrying out more attacks. The fight against ISIS isn't over, but governments around the world will continue fighting for as long as it takes to keep their citizens safe.

How You See History

1. Why was losing control of Dabiq such a major loss for ISIS, even though it was a relatively small area of land?
2. Why was ISIS not really defeated, even after it had lost all of its lands?
3. What do you think world leaders can do to stop ISIS from regaining its strength in the Middle East and around the world?

TIMELINE

2004

Abu Musab al-Zarqawi establishes al-Qaeda in Iraq (AQI).

2006

Al-Zarqawi is killed in a U.S. air strike, and Abu Ayyub al-Masri takes his place as leader of AQI; al-Masri announces the creation of the Islamic State of Iraq (ISI) and declares Abu Omar al-Baghdadi the commander of the faithful.

2010

Abu Bakr al-Baghdadi becomes leader of ISI when al-Masri and Abu Omar al-Baghdadi are killed in an operation led by the United States and Iraq.

2013

ISI tries to absorb the al-Nusra Front in Syria, but the al-Nusra Front resists; Abu Bakr al-Baghdadi establishes the Islamic State in Iraq and Syria (ISIS).

2014

Al-Qaeda renounces ties to the Islamic State; ISIS takes control of Mosul and Fallujah in Iraq; Abu Bakr al-Baghdadi declares himself caliph in a videotaped sermon on July 4; a global coalition is formed to fight ISIS.

2015

ISIS followers launch a series of coordinated terrorist attacks in Paris, France, on November 13; on December 2, ISIS supporters carry out a mass shooting at an office Christmas party in San Bernardino, California.

2016

Supporters of ISIS carry out terrorist attacks in Brussels, Berlin, Jakarta, and Orlando, among other cities; ISIS loses control of the cities of Ramadi and Fallujah in Iraq and Dabiq in Syria.

2017

ISIS claims responsibility for major terrorist attacks in England, Iran, and Egypt; Mosul is taken back by Iraqi forces in July; Raqqa is taken back by Syrian forces in October.

2019

ISIS followers attack a number of targets in Sri Lanka, killing more than 300 people; the last official piece of ISIS territory in Syria is lost in March; Abu Bakr al-Baghdadi kills himself to avoid being captured by U.S. forces on October 26.

2021

ISIS claims responsibility for suicide bombings at a Baghdad market in January that leave more than 30 people dead.

NOTES

Introduction: The Islamic State

1. Quoted in Peter Baker, Eric Schmitt, and Helene Cooper, "ISIS Leader al-Baghdadi Is Dead, Trump Says," *New York Times*, October 27, 2019, www.nytimes.com/2019/10/27/us/politics/isis-leader-al-baghdadi-dead.html.

Chapter One: Al-Qaeda in Iraq

1. Quoted in "Egyptian Doctor Emerges as Terror Mastermind," CNN, 2005, www.cnn.com/CNN/Programs/people/shows/zawahiri/profile.html.
2. Quoted in Mary Anne Weaver, "The Short, Violent Life of Abu Musab al-Zarqawi," *Atlantic*, June 8, 2006, www.theatlantic.com/magazine/archive/2006/07/the-short-violent-life-of-abu-musab-al-zarqawi/304983/.
3. Quoted in Weaver, "The Short, Violent Life of Abu Musab al-Zarqawi."
4. Quoted in Weaver, "The Short, Violent Life of Abu Musab al-Zarqawi."
5. Quoted in Weaver, "The Short, Violent Life of Abu Musab al-Zarqawi."

Chapter Two: From AQI to ISI

1. Quoted in William McCants, "State of Confusion: ISIS' Strategy and How to Counter It," The Brookings Institution, September 11, 2014, www.brookings.edu/opinions/state-of-confusion-isis-strategy-and-how-to-counter-it/.

Chapter Three: A New Leader

1. Quoted in William McCants, "The Believer: How an Introvert with a Passion for Religion and Soccer Became Abu Bakr al-Baghdadi: Leader of the Islamic State," The Brookings Institution, September 1, 2015, csweb.brookings.edu/content/research/essays/2015/thebeliever.html.
2. McCants, "The Believer."
3. Quoted in McCants, "The Believer."

Chapter Four: Creating the Caliphate

1. Quoted in "Profile: Syria's al-Nusra Front," BBC, April 10, 2013, www.bbc.com/news/world-middle-east-18048033.
2. Quoted in William McCants, *The ISIS Apocalypse: The History, Strategy, and Doomsday Vision of the Islamic State* (New York, NY: St. Martin's Press, 2015), p. 98.
3. Quoted in Liz Sly and Ahmed Ramadan, "Insurgents Seize Iraqi City of Mosul as Security Forces Flee," *Washington Post*, June 10, 2014, www.washingtonpost.com/world/insurgents-seize-iraqi-city-of-mosul-as-troops-flee/2014/06/10/21061e87-8fcd-4ed3-bc94-0e309af0a674_story.html.
4. Quoted in Chelsea J. Carter and Hamdi Alkhshali, "Video Emerges of Purported Militant Leader in Mosul Preaching Holy War," CNN, July 5, 2014, www.cnn.com/2014/07/05/world/meast/iraq-crisis/.
5. Quoted in William McCants, "The Believer: How an Introvert with a Passion for Religion and Soccer Became Abu Bakr al-Baghdadi: Leader of the Islamic State," The Brookings Institution, September 1, 2015, csweb.brookings.edu/content/research/essays/2015/thebeliever.html.
6. Graeme Wood, "What ISIS Really Wants," *Atlantic*, March 2015, www.theatlantic.com/magazine/archive/2015/03/what-isis-really-wants/384980/.
7. Quoted in Wood, "What ISIS Really Wants."
8. Quoted in Rick Noack, "The ISIS Apocalypse Has Been Postponed but the Militants Might Still Believe in It," *Washington Post*, October 17, 2016, www.washingtonpost.com/news/worldviews/wp/2016/10/17/the-isis-apocalypse-has-been-postponed-but-the-militants-might-still-believe-in-it/?utm_term=.651bccd609c0.

Chapter Five: Life Under ISIS Control

1. Quoted in William McCants, *The ISIS Apocalypse: The History, Strategy, and Doomsday Vision of the Islamic State* (New York, NY: St. Martin's Press, 2015), p. 104.
2. Quoted in Mariam Karouny, "Apocalyptic Prophecies Drive Both Sides to Syrian Battle for End of Time," Reuters, April 1, 2014, www.reuters.com/article/us-syria-crisis-prophecy-insight-idUSBREA3013420140401.

3. Quoted in Michael Weiss and Hassan Hassan, *ISIS: Inside the Army of Terror* (New York, NY: Simon and Schuster, 2015), p. xii.
4. Quoted in Graeme Wood, "What ISIS Really Wants," *Atlantic*, March 2015, www.theatlantic.com/magazine/archive/2015/03/what-isis-really-wants/384980/.
5. Kimberly Dozier, "They Were Children When They Were Kidnapped by ISIS and Forced to Fight. What Happens Now That They're Home?" *TIME*, May 23, 2019, time.com/longform/isis-child-soldiers-yezidi/.
6. Quoted in Susannah Cullinane, Hamdi Alkhshali, and Mohammed Tawfeeq, "Tracking a Trail of Historical Obliteration: ISIS Trumpets Destruction of Nimrud," CNN, April 13, 2015, www.cnn.com/2015/03/09/world/iraq-isis-heritage/.
7. Quoted in Cullinane, Alkhshali, and Tawfeeq, "ISIS Trumpets Destruction of Nimrud."

Chapter Six: A Global Threat

1. Quoted in Sam Jones, Angelique Chrisafis, and Caroline Davies, "Nice Truck Attack: Islamic State Claims Responsibility," *Guardian*, July 16, 2016, www.theguardian.com/world/2016/jul/16/islamic-state-claims-responsibility-for-nice-truck-attack.
2. Quoted in Kate Samuelson and Jared Malsin, "ISIS Claims Responsibility for Manchester Concert Terrorist Attack," *TIME*, May 23, 2017, time.com/4790201/isis-manchester-concert-terrorist-attack/.

Chapter Seven: The Future of ISIS

1. Jane Ferguson, "Why the Human Toll of the Battle for Mosul May Never Be Known," *PBS NewsHour*, December 19, 2018, www.pbs.org/newshour/show/why-the-human-toll-of-the-battle-for-mosul-may-never-be-known.
2. Quoted in Ruth Sherlock, Lama Al-Arian, and Kamiran Sadoun, "'This Is Not Liberation': Life in the Rubble of Raqqa, Syria," NPR, October 26, 2018, www.npr.org/2018/10/26/658142688/u-s-plan-to-stabilize-raqqa-and-stop-return-of-isis-doesnt-appear-to-be-working.

FOR MORE INFORMATION

Books: Nonfiction

Bailey, Diane. *Rescue from an ISIS Prison! Delta Force in Iraq During the War on Terror*. Broomall, PA: Mason Crest, 2019.

Croy, Anita. *Terrorism: Are We All at Risk?* New York, NY: Lucent Press, 2020.

Heing, Bridey. *Investigating Terrorist Attacks at the Hands of ISIS*. New York, NY: Rosen Young Adult, 2018.

Lawrence, Blythe. *War and Terrorism in the Twenty-First Century*. San Diego, CA: ReferencePoint Press, 2020.

Marsico, Katie. *ISIS*. Minneapolis, MN: Abdo Publishing, 2016.

Townsend, Chris. *The Violent Rise of ISIS*. New York, NY: Enslow Publishing, 2018.

Books: Fiction

Abawi, Atia. *A Land of Permanent Goodbyes*. New York, NY: Philomel Books, 2018.

Myers, Walter Dean. *Sunrise Over Fallujah*. New York, NY: Scholastic, 2008.

Websites

CNN: ISIS Fast Facts

www.cnn.com/2014/08/08/world/isis-fast-facts/index.html

CNN's website has a detailed page about ISIS, featuring important facts about the organization and a timeline of its actions and attacks.

Nadia's Initiative

www.nadiasinitiative.org

The official website for Nadia Murad's activist work provides information about her story as a Yazidi woman captured by ISIS and her work raising awareness about the crimes ISIS has committed against the Yazidi people.

The Secret History of ISIS

www.pbs.org/wgbh/frontline/film/the-secret-history-of-isis

This website has a link to a film featured on the PBS series *Frontline*, which details the creation and rise of the Islamic State.

Timeline: The Rise, Spread, and Fall of the Islamic State

www.wilsoncenter.org/article/timeline-the-rise-spread-and-fall-the-islamic-state

This timeline is a detailed list of many of the important dates and events in the history of ISIS.

UNESCO: Revive the Spirit of Mosul

en.unesco.org/fieldoffice/baghdad/revivemosul

The official website for the Revive the Spirit of Mosul project includes information about how UNESCO is working to restore the cultural and historical identity of this Iraqi city.

INDEX

PHOTO CREDITS

Cover SOPA Images/Contributor/LightRocket/Getty Images; p. 4 Handout/Handout/Getty Images News/Getty Images; pp. 8, 20, 58, 70 Anadolu Agency/Contributor/Anadolu Agency/Getty Images; p. 10 Jeff J Mitchell/Staff/Getty Images News/Getty Images; p. 12 Getty Images/Stringer/Getty Images News/Getty Images; p. 15 Robert Nickelsberg/Contributor/Hulton Archive/Getty Images; p. 17 KHALIL MAZRAAWI/Stringer/AFP/Getty Images; p. 21 New York Daily News Archive/Contributor/New York Daily News/Getty Images; p. 26 AHMAD AL-RUBAYE/Stringer/AFP/Getty Images; pp. 29, 53 PeterHermesFurian/iStock/Getty Images Plus/Getty Images; p. 30 Chris Hondros/Staff/Getty Images News/Getty Images; p. 36 Universal History Archive/Contributor/Universal Images Group/Getty Images; p. 38 PRAKASH SINGH/Staff/AFP/Getty Images; p. 41 DAVID FURST/Contributor/AFP/Getty Images; p. 44 rasoul ali/Moment/Getty Images; p. 47 SAFIN HAMED/Contributor/AFP/Getty Images; pp. 48, 57 NurPhoto/Contributor/NurPhoto/Getty Images; p. 51 LOUAI BESHARA/Staff/AFP/Getty Images; p. 61 The White House/Handout/Getty Images News/Getty Images; p. 62 BULENT KILIC/Contributor/AFP/Getty Images; p. 65 STR/Stringer/AFP/Getty Images; p. 68 DELIL SOULEIMAN/Contributor/AFP/Getty Images; p. 71 JOSEPH EID/Stringer/AFP/Getty Images; p. 74 JOHN THYS/Stringer/AFP/Getty Images; p. 76 Drew Angerer/Staff/Getty Images News/Getty Images; p. 79 PHILIPPE WOJAZER/Staff/AFP/Getty Images; p. 82 THOMAS SAMSON/Contributor/AFP/Getty Images; p. 84 FADEL SENNA/Contributor/AFP/Getty Images; p. 87 AHMAD AL-RUBAYE/Contributor/AFP/Getty Images; p. 88 Rune Hellestad - Corbis/Contributor/Corbis Entertainment/Getty Images; p. 90 (top) GIUSEPPE CACACE/Contributor/AFP/Getty Images; p. 90 (bottom) AAREF WATAD/Contributor/AFP/Getty Images.

ABOUT THE AUTHOR

Joseph Stanley is the author of several books for children and young adults. He is a passionate history buff who enjoys learning about military strategy in the past and present. His other interests include taking long road trips every spring, playing baseball, and supporting his beloved Buffalo Bills. He lives in Western New York with his family, but his heart is always at the beach.